BRN TO COOK
Angel Food

written by
Joyce Molyneux and Gerard Baker

for Save the Children

Save the Children works in more than 120 countries.

We save children's lives.

We fight for their rights.

We help them fulfil their potential.

Published by Adam White

Photography by Michael Murray King and Adam White

Edited by Michael Weare

Designed by Mark Griffiths

First published in 2011 by Adam White (Impact Printing Services Ltd. 07557 042 417)

© Text by Adam White and Gerard Baker

© Photographs by Adam White

Home economy and food styling by Gerard Baker and Meriel Matthews

isbn number 978-0-9570314-0-1

Printed by The Westdale Press Limited

70 Portmanmoor Ind. Est,

East Moors, Cardiff CF24 5HB

For Meriel Matthews, our friend and colleague for so many years. The success of this book depends on her energy and enthusiasm both for food and her beloved cause, Save the Children.

Foreword

If anyone was born to cook, my God, Joyce Molyneux was. The woman is a legend among cooks, restaurateurs and foodies. Her first cookbook sold fifty thousand copies; her restaurant, the Carved Angel, which she owned and cooked in for twenty years, had a Michelin Star and a world-wide reputation; she spawned shoals of good cooks who went on to be culinary stars, and her food delights today as it did fifty years ago. She and her co-author, fellow chef, disciple and friend Gerard Baker, have ever been true to the classic principles of Elizabeth David: good fresh ingredients; local produce, seasonal food, great flavour, no pretention.

She's eighty now, and unstoppable. This book, I confess, gave me a sinking feeling, a frisson of apprehension, the fear that it might be so damn good that no one would buy the *Leith's Cookery Bible* any more. For *Born to Cook* is a bible. It has everything you might want in it - instructions for simple tasks like using split peas and making chutney, to grilling lobster or prepping lambs' sweetbreads to nestle seductively in a puff pastry case, wallowing in a sorrel cream sauce. O Yum.

The book is admirably eclectic. Joyce never saw herself as a bastion of British cooking, nor single-mindedly into classic French cuisine, nor a fashionable follower of the latest Thai or Tuscan fad. She just loves good food, wherever she encounters it. So some of the recipes are for Far Eastern dishes, many for European dishes, especially Mediterranean ones, and of course plenty are good old British favourites.

For years in the less busy months, Joyce ran classes in the kitchens of the Carved Angel, teaching her customers and others to cook. But she also spent a lot of her time on what used to be called "good works," (now, less forthrightly, "working with disadvantaged communities"). She has taught countless children and young chefs to plant and tend vegetables and herbs and then to cook with the fruits of their labours.

There is no more effective way of tackling the twin horrors of modern times: obesity and starvation, than to teach the world to grow and cook. The recipes in this book have been tried and tested in both the domestic and restaurant settings; they reflect the truth that food education is not confined to nutrition, food production or politics, but is mainly taught in the allotment and kitchen.

Which of course is how it should be. How can we expect parents to pass on their culture and mores to their children if they never sit down to eat with them, if the family members pass each other as they collect their separate ready meals, microwave them and then head for their bedrooms or studies or flop silent in front of the TV.

How can we stem the tide of ill-health, eating disorders and unhappiness if we do not teach our children how to eat? And the way to do that is to cook good food with them, then sit down with them and enjoy it.

I am sure most of the people who buy this book will do so because they are keen cooks. Personally I want to cook everything in it. But I would like to see it under the Christmas tree for every family in Britain too. Not just because between its covers lies a cornucopia of pleasure, but also because the profits go to Save the Children's wonderful campaign, No Child Born to Die, with its corollary of every child born to shine, to run, to play, to write, and lots else. And, I fervently hope, to cook.

Prue Leith

Introduction

The success of any restaurant relies not just on good chefs and good recipes: excellent suppliers and willing customers are essential too. The Carved Angel in Dartmouth brought together these elements over 20 years of successful trading and its recipes live on in the kitchens of the many chefs who trained with Joyce Molyneux, and in the memories of its many devoted suppliers and customers.

A pioneer of seasonal food, locally sourced from dozens of small suppliers, Joyce created a unique, ever-changing menu that was flexible enough to absorb ingredients no matter how small or fleeting the supply. Local customers knew that she would jump at the chance to buy mulberries, figs, the odd mackerel or a basketful of chanterelles, and the bounty of South Devon fuelled her cooking.

Joyce arrived in Dartmouth from Bath, where she had worked and been a partner for many years at The Hole in the Wall with George Perry Smith. Here the chefs cooked with Elizabeth David in mind and brought Mediterranean food to a new audience.

In her own kitchen, Joyce's love of food took on new dimensions, and included recipes and ideas from many other food writers from the middle and far east, and the food in this book reflects her willingness to experiment and adapt. Her colleagues Tom Jaine, Meriel Matthews and Nick Coiley and the many staff at the restaurant all contributed hugely to the restaurant's success. For her brilliance, Joyce was one of the first women anywhere to be awarded a Michelin Star.

The recipes in this book have been selected by Joyce and her friend, the chef and writer Gerard Baker, who has adapted the text to suit today's kitchens. Good recipes are timeless – chefs adopt them, amend and alter – then pass them on to a new audience. You should feel, as you cook, that you can alter them to suit your own taste – no one should follow them slavishly.

It is simply hoped that you enjoy cooking and eating them, just as the many chefs and customers of The Carved Angel did for so many years.

Joyce Molyneux and Gerard Baker

Soups

Vegetables

Pasta and rice

Fish and shellfish

Poultry

Meat and game

Bakery

Desserts

Soups

The selection of soups in this chapter ranges from the very light to the substantial and luxurious, and reflects the varied way that soups can be used in your repertoire. We find that soup makes a quick and easy lunch that can be both restoring and comforting. Accompanied by bread and perhaps with some cheese and fruit to follow, a soup can make a complete meal.

In this chapter you will find subtly spiced winter soups such as carrot and coriander, and parsnip and apple, both of which have deep, long flavours that will satisfy on a chilly day. Watercress, equally, is a winter vegetable that can be used to make a very fine and delicate soup to serve at a dinner party. Meat soups are less common today than they used to be, but readers will find the split pea and ham soup and the game consommé both delicious and economical ways of maximising the flavour of simple ingredients.

Of the summer soups, the three chilled ones in this chapter stand out. The two Spanish soups come from Joyce's time on holiday in Andalusia. Both are well worth trying, while the Hungarian Morello cherry soup can be served both as a starter or a dessert.

The key to making soups taste really delicious is to use good ingredients, cook them expertly and to use only good, home-made stocks. To this end, we have included several basic recipes for you to use. Keep stock in the freezer, and you can make a batch of soup easily at any time.

Cherry soup

Morello cherries are a special delight, but are a rarity fresh. They can be bought frozen from one or two supermarkets, which although is not quite the same as having them from a tree, is an acceptable substitute. This lovely recipe is a straight take from Victor Sassie via Jane Grigson and perfect for a warm summer's day lunch.

Serves 4-6

method

Stone the cherries over a medium stainless steel saucepan so as not to waste any of the juices, and set the fruit aside. To the juice in the pan, add the stones and any stalks you have along with the sugar and the wine. Bring these to a boil over a medium to high heat, and simmer for about five minutes. Strain the liquid into a clean pan. It will have absorbed a wonderful colour and flavour from the stones.

Add the cinnamon, lemon zest and lemon juice to the pan and bring back to a simmer. Add the cherries and any more juice that has collected. Bring the pan to a rolling boil and immediately remove from the heat. Allow the soup to cool slightly and stir in the brandy. Put the cream into a large bowl and slowly whisk in the soup, holding back the cherries until the mixture is smooth. Then tip in the cherries and stir. When cool, chill in the fridge and serve very cold.

Note: if you prefer a thicker soup, liquidize half the cherries until smooth, then sieve into the remaining soup.

ingredients

450g Morello cherries
55g sugar
750ml bottle medium-dry Riesling
Pinch cinnamon
Zest of 1 lemon, grated
Juice of 2 lemons
30ml brandy
600ml soured cream

Parsnip and apple soup

The mellow, nutty flavour of parsnips deepens in the winter, and is lightened in this soup with a touch of apple.

Serves 4-6

method

In a large pan, melt the butter over a low to medium heat and add the onion, apple and parsnips. Cook gently, covered, for ten minutes, stirring occasionally to make sure nothing is sticking. Add the curry powder, stock and seasoning, and simmer over a medium heat for about 20 minutes until the vegetables are soft. Put the soup in a liquidizer and blend it in batches until it is very smooth and fine. Pour the soup back into the pan through a fine sieve and add the cream. Heat, stirring, until almost boiling and season to taste with salt and pepper.

ingredients

25g unsalted butter

1 onion, peeled and roughly chopped

225g cooking apple, peeled and sliced

225g parsnips, peeled and sliced

2 tsp curry powder

1.4 litres chicken or vegetable stock (page 31 or 33)

300ml single cream

Salt and freshly ground black pepper

Tomato and orange soup

In the late summer, ripe tomatoes can often be bought for a song from local growers keen to clear their crop. The deep ripe flavour marries well with the freshness of the orange.

Serves 4

method

In a large pan melt the butter over a low to medium heat. Add the onions and the garlic and let them cook gently until they are beginning to soften, but do not let them brown. Wash the tomatoes, cut them roughly, and add them to the pan along with the orange peel and a little salt and pepper. Cover and cook for 30 minutes over a low heat, squashing the tomatoes from time to time. Put the soup into a liquidizer and blend it in batches until very smooth, then pass through a mouli or a sieve to remove any bits of skin.

If the soup is very thick, you can thin it with a little vegetable stock (page 33) or water. Season to taste, adding a pinch of sugar if necessary, and serve with whipped cream and some chopped tarragon on top.

ingredients

55g unsalted butter

2 large onions, peeled and roughly chopped

2 cloves of garlic, peeled and roughly chopped

900g very ripe tomatoes

Strip of orange peel without the white pith

Salt and freshly ground black pepper

½ tsp sugar to taste

French tarragon leaves and a little whipped cream to serve

Chilled Andalusian almond and grape soup

Muscat grapes – also sold as Italia grapes - come onto the market in late September. Their scent is special and unique and they are well worth hunting out for this lovely late summer treat. It is important to use high quality ingredients for this simple soup, including good bread and equally good oil.

Serves 4

method

First blanch the almonds. Place the nuts in a small pan and cover with water. Bring to a boil over a high heat and cook for two minutes. Drain and cover the nuts with cold water. Peel the almonds, discarding the brown skins, and dry the white kernels on kitchen paper.

Slice the garlic and put it into a food processor with the almonds. Squeeze out the bread, add to the garlic and nuts and blend to a smooth paste. Add the oil, vinegar and seasoning and blend again. Now dilute with cold water to a thin, creamy consistency. Check the seasoning, as it may need a little more vinegar. Pour into a bowl, add the grapes and serve immediately.

ingredients

200g whole almonds, skin on

4 cloves of garlic, peeled

200g white country bread without crusts, soaked in water for an hour or so

600-850ml water, as required

125ml extra virgin olive oil

4 tbsp tarragon vinegar, or white wine vinegar

Salt and freshly ground black pepper

225g grapes, Muscat if possible, peeled and halved, to serve

Borscht

The velvet richness of beetroot is special and yet this soup is light with its addition of apple. We used to serve this soup with little pastries filled with mushrooms for a light lunch (see below).

Serves 4

method

In a large pan, heat 2 tbsp duck or pork fat over a low to medium heat. Add the onions, garlic and chopped celery and sauté gently in a covered pan for about ten minutes. Do not allow the vegetables to colour, turn the heat down if necessary. Add the apple, beetroot, stock and seasoning to the pan, bring to the boil over a high heat and simmer gently for 15-20 minutes until all the vegetables are tender. Add the gherkin and season to taste with a little lemon juice or vinegar. Serve with a dollop of soured cream and mushroom turnovers on the side.

ingredients

A little duck or pork fat or dripping

1 large onion, peeled and chopped

1 clove garlic, peeled and chopped

1 stick celery, washed and chopped

55g cooking apple, peeled and chopped

725g raw beetroot, trimmed, washed and coarsely grated

1.2 litres duck, pork or chicken stock (page 31)

1 large gherkin finely chopped

Lemon juice or vinegar to taste

Salt and freshly ground black pepper

125ml soured cream to serve

Mushroom turnovers

Start by making a batch of shortcrust pastry with 200g plain flour and 100g unsalted butter (see page 113).

Serves 4

method

Heat the butter in a medium pan over a medium heat and add the onions. Stir, cooking for a couple of minutes. While the onion cooks, finely chop the mushrooms in a food processor and add to the pan. Simmer for five to ten minutes over a medium heat until the mixture is dry, stirring constantly. Add the parsley and seasoning to taste, then allow to cool.

Preheat the oven to 200C/Gas mark 6.

Roll out the pastry to a thickness of about 3mm and cut into 12cm circles. Divide the mushroom mixture between the rounds and fold the pastry over to make little crescents. Seal the edges with a little egg wash. Place the pastries onto baking trays lined with non-stick baking paper and brush them with the rest of the egg to glaze. Bake for 10-15 minutes until well browned. Cool a little before serving with the borscht.

ingredients

25g butter

1 large onion, peeled and finely chopped

225g mushrooms, cleaned and finely chopped

1 small bunch flat-leaf parsley, washed, dried and chopped

Salt and freshly ground black pepper

1 egg, beaten, to glaze

Watercress soup

If you are lucky enough to have a patch of sorrel in your garden, this soup could also be made with a large handful of sorrel in place of half the watercress. The sorrel has a super, sharp tang but loses its colour quickly, so is best used in concert with watercress.

Serves 4

method

Trim the watercress so that you have the leaves in one pile and the stalks in another. Melt the butter in a large pan over a low to medium heat and add the onions. Sauté gently for about five minutes and then add the watercress stalks, potato, stock and a little salt and pepper. Bring the soup to a boil over a high heat and simmer gently for 20 minutes or until the potato is soft. Add the watercress leaves, put the soup into a liquidizer and blend in batches until very smooth, then pass through a fine sieve into a clean pan. Add the cream and the nutmeg and bring the soup back to a light simmer. Be careful not to overheat the soup at this stage or you will diminish both its colour and flavour. Check the seasoning and serve.

ingredients

250g watercress (about 2 large bunches)

25g butter

2 large onions, peeled and roughly chopped

175g potato, peeled and diced finely

1.2 litres chicken or vegetable stock (page 31 or 33)

150ml single cream

Salt, freshly ground black pepper and nutmeg to taste

Game consommé

This light but flavoursome soup ideally needs to be made over two days. First the stock is made, simmered gently to maintain clarity. The next day, when the stock is chilled, all traces of fat need to be removed to give a clear, brilliant result. To do this, egg white is added, which will pick up every trace of sediment. The soup is excellent served with little game turnovers.

Serves 6-8

method

Preheat the oven to 220C/Gas mark 8.

Toss the bones in a large bowl with a little sunflower oil and place in a large roasting tin so that the bones are in a single layer. Roast the bones for thirty minutes, turning them halfway through, until they are well browned. Pour off any excess fat.

Heat the dripping in a large pan over a medium to high heat and add the vegetables. Sauté them, stirring, until they are well browned. Add the herbs and peppercorns, and mix well. Add the stock, the wine, the purée and the roasted bones, turn the heat to high and bring almost to a boil. Then turn the heat to very low and simmer without boiling for two hours.

Strain the liquid into a bowl through a very fine sieve. When it is cool, chill, preferably overnight, then scrape all the fat from the surface, using kitchen paper to wipe the surface clean if it is jellied.

Return the soup to a clean saucepan. Lightly beat the egg white and whisk it thoroughly into the soup with a little salt. Place the pan over a high heat and warm until it just beings to simmer. At that point, turn the heat to very low and allow a crust of egg white to form for about 15 minutes. Then strain the soup carefully through a sieve lined with muslin. Check the seasoning and serve the consommé alongside the game turnovers (see page 27).

ingredients

1.3kg game and pork bones (including giblets and a pigs trotter if available)

A little sunflower oil

40g dripping

4 large onions, peeled and roughly chopped

225g carrot, washed, peeled and roughly chopped

2 sticks celery, washed and chopped

Small bunch each fresh thyme, parsley and marjoram

2 bay leaves

10 black peppercorns

2.25 litres dark chicken stock (see page 31)

300ml red wine

2 tsp tomato purée

1 egg white

Game turnovers

Start by making a batch of shortcrust pastry with 200g plain flour and 100g unsalted butter (see page 113).

Serves 4

method

Melt the butter in a medium pan over a medium heat. Add the onion and garlic, and sauté, stirring for five minutes without colouring. Add the mushrooms and cook, stirring, then add the port and simmer to reduce until the mixture is fairly dry. Add the meat and sauté gently until it is cooked through. Taste and season assertively, then allow the mixture to cool.

 Preheat the oven to 220C/Gas mark 7

Roll out the pastry to a thickness of about 3mm and cut into 12cm circles. Divide the filling between the rounds and fold the pastry over to make little crescents. Seal the edges with a little egg wash. Place the pastries onto baking trays lined with non-stick baking paper and brush them with rest of the egg to glaze. Bake for 10-15 minutes until well browned and cooked through. Cool a little before serving with the consommé.

ingredients

15g butter

1 small onion, peeled and finely chopped

½ clove garlic, peeled and finely chopped

115g mushrooms, wiped and finely chopped

75ml port

115g minced game meat (venison, wild duck or hare)

Milk to glaze

Salt and freshly ground black pepper

Scallop and artichoke chowder

An increasing number of people are diving for scallops around our coastline and will send them to you in the post the next day.

This soup is best made and eaten immediately, but if you need to you can cook it up to the point where you are ready to fry the scallops, and then chill it. When you are ready to serve you can fry the scallops and reheat the soup at the same time. This rich soup is best served before a light main course, or as a lunch or supper dish.

method

Melt half the butter in a pan and sweat the vegetables gently for five minutes. Add the stock, wine and seasoning and cook for another 20 minutes. In a separate pan, fry the scallops in the rest of the butter. Add the vegetable and stock mixture to the scallops and bring to a simmer over a high heat. To finish the soup, add the cream, let it come back to a light simmer, then season to taste with a little lemon juice and parsley.

Serve with hot, crisp buttered toast.

ingredients

55g unsalted butter

2 large or 3 medium onions, peeled and finely diced

225g Jerusalem artichokes, washed, peeled and finely diced

225g potato, washed, peeled and finely diced

700ml chicken stock or light fish stock (see page 31 or 32)

150ml dry, light white wine

8 large scallops, cleaned and trimmed, cut into chunks

150ml double cream

Lemon juice to taste

Small bunch flat-leaf parsley, chopped

Salt and freshly ground black pepper

Spinach and coconut soup

Spinach has a velvety richness when puréed which is enhanced by the subtle flavour of coconut in this lovely soup.

Serves 4

method

Melt the butter in a large pan over a low to medium heat. Add the onion and sauté for five minutes without colouring. Add the spinach, rice, liquid and a little seasoning. Raise the heat and bring the soup to a simmer. Add the creamed coconut then reduce the heat and simmer gently for 15 minutes or until the rice is tender. Remove from the heat and allow to cool slightly. Put the soup into a liquidizer and blend in batches until very smooth, then pass through a mouli or a sieve into a clean pan. Add the cream and reheat gently, and season with a little salt, pepper and nutmeg.

ingredients

25g butter

2 large onions, peeled and roughly chopped

450g spinach, washed and drained

25g white rice

1.2 litres light chicken stock (see page 31) or water

25g creamed coconut

125ml single cream

Salt, freshly ground black pepper and nutmeg to taste

Split pea and ham soup

This economical soup balances the earthy sweet flavour of the peas with the clean salty tang of the ham: it is truly delicious. Split peas have a tendency to sink to the bottom of the pan as they cook, so keep an eye on them and stir the pan regularly to prevent them sticking.

Serves 6

method

Melt the butter in a large pan over a low to medium heat. Add the onions and sauté, stirring for five minutes. Add the split peas, stock, celery and garlic. Reduce the heat to low, cover the pan and simmer gently for an hour to an hour and a half. Put the soup into a liquidizer and blend in batches until very smooth, then return to a clean pan. Finish off by adding the cream and ham, diced or shredded, and season to taste. Serve with croutons.

ingredients

55g butter

2 large onions, peeled and finely chopped

225g yellow split peas

1.4 litres stock - ham or vegetable stock (see page 33)

1 stick celery, washed and finely chopped

1 clove garlic, peeled and finely chopped

150ml single cream

100g cooked ham left over from a joint, or cooked ham hock

Salt, freshly ground black pepper and nutmeg to taste

Carrot and coriander soup

These two flavours marry well to create an earthy, substantial soup.

Serves 4

method

Melt the butter in a pan over a low to medium heat. Add the carrot, onion and coriander, and cook gently, covered, for 10-15 minutes. Stir occasionally to ensure that the vegetables are not sticking to the pan – if they are, turn down the heat. Add the stock and a little salt and pepper, then cover and cook gently for another 30 minutes. Put the soup into a liquidizer and blend in batches, until very smooth, then pass it through a mouli or a sieve back into a clean pan. Add the cream and check the seasoning. Serve immediately.

ingredients

55g butter

450g carrots, washed, peeled and thinly sliced

1 large onion, peeled and roughly chopped

2 tsp freshly ground coriander seed

1.2 litres chicken or vegetable stock (page 31 or 33)

150ml single cream

Salt and freshly ground black pepper

Gazpacho

When made with the sweetest tomatoes and thoroughly chilled, this soup cannot be beaten on a hot day – it is so refreshing.

Serves 4

method

Put all the ingredients in a liquidizer and blend until very smooth with a little salt and pepper. Pass through a fine sieve and dilute with a little ice or water to a consistency you like. Taste the soup, adding seasoning to your own taste and serve with the egg, cucumber, spring onion and garlic croutons in little bowls for your guests to help themselves.

ingredients

900g very ripe tomatoes, sliced, all juices reserved

175g red peppers deseeded and sliced

1 clove garlic, peeled and sliced

55ml extra virgin olive oil

25ml vinegar

A few basil or tarragon leaves, chopped

Salt and freshly ground black pepper

Chopped hard boiled egg, diced peeled cucumber, chopped spring onions and garlic croutons to serve

Chicken stock

Makes 2 litres

method

Place all the ingredients in a large pan and add 2 litres cold water. Place the pan on a medium heat and bring it to a simmer very slowly – do not allow the stock to boil. Cook at a low simmer for two hours, then strain through a fine sieve into a large bowl, discarding the debris. When the stock is cool, cover it and chill, then remove and discard any fat that has risen to the surface.

The stock will keep for one week in the fridge or two months in the freezer.

ingredients

1kg raw chicken carcasses or wings

2 onions, peeled and sliced

1 carrot, peeled and sliced

1 stick celery, washed and roughly chopped

Small bunch parsley

1 large sprig fresh thyme

3 bay leaves

1 tsp black peppercorns

Dark chicken stock

Makes 2 litres

method

Place the raw chicken carcasses in a large roasting tin and cook in an oven preheated to 220C/Gas mark 7 for 30 minutes. Reduce the heat to 180C/Gas mark 4 for a further hour until the bones are an even, deep brown and all the fat has rendered from them. Drain off and discard the fat, then pour one litre of water into the roasting tin and let it sit for ten minutes while you prepare the vegetables.

Put the vegetables and another litre of cold water in a large pan. Add the chicken carcasses and the liquid from the roasting tin, scraping out all the caramelised bits, and all the remaining ingredients. Place the pan over a low heat, let it come up to a gentle simmer and allow it to cook for two hours without boiling. Strain the stock through a fine sieve into a large bowl and discard the debris. When the stock is cool, cover it and chill, then remove and discard any fat that has risen to the surface.

The stock will keep for one week in the fridge or two months in the freezer.

ingredients

As for Chicken Stock (see above)

Note: to make a game stock, replace the chicken bones with game bones. To make a jellied chicken or game stock, add a raw, split pigs trotter to the pan as you put the stock to simmer. It will lend body to the stock.

Meat stock

Makes 2 litres

method

Place the bones in a large roasting tin and cook in an oven preheated to 220C/Gas mark 7 for 30 minutes. Reduce the heat to 180C/Gas mark 4 for a further hour until the bones are an even, deep brown and all the fat has rendered from them. Drain off the fat and reserve for your store cupboard, then pour one litre water into the roasting tin and let it sit for ten minutes while you prepare the vegetables.

Put the vegetables and another litre of cold water in a large pan. Add the bones and the liquid from the roasting tin, scraping out all the caramelised bits, and all the remaining ingredients. Place the pan over a low heat, let it come up to a gentle simmer and allow it to cook for two hours without boiling. Strain the stock through a fine sieve into a large bowl and discard the debris. When the stock is cool, cover it and chill, then remove and store any fat that has risen to the surface.

The stock will keep for one week in the fridge or two months in the freezer.

ingredients

1.5kg beef, lamb or pork bones

2 onions, peeled and sliced

1 carrot, peeled and sliced

1 stick celery, washed and chopped

Small bunch parsley

1 large sprig fresh thyme

2 bay leaves

1 tsp black peppercorns

Fish stock

Makes 2 litres

For best results use the bones and trimmings of white fish or salmon. To make a shellfish stock, replace the fish trimmings with shellfish bones or prawn shells and add a chopped tomato.

method

Put all the ingredients in a large pan over a medium to high heat and cover with 2 litres of cold water. Bring the pan to a simmer for 30 minutes, then remove from the heat and strain the stock through a fine sieve. Allow to cool, then chill and keep for up to four days in the fridge or up to one month in the freezer.

ingredients

1kg fish trimmings

1 onion, peeled and sliced

1 stick celery, washed and chopped

1 small bunch fresh parsley

1 sprig thyme

1 bay leaf

1 tsp white peppercorns

Vegetable stock

Makes 1 litre

method

Place all the ingredients in a large pan and cover with 1 litre of cold water. Bring to a simmer over a high heat, then reduce the heat to low and simmer for one hour. Strain through a fine sieve and cool. When cold, the stock will keep for up to one week in the fridge or one month in the freezer.

ingredients

4 onions, peeled and sliced

2 carrots, peeled and sliced

2 sticks celery, peeled and sliced

1 bulb fennel, washed and chopped

2 cloves garlic, peeled and sliced

1 tsp black peppercorns

Vegetables

No longer are vegetables seen only as accompaniments, to be boiled and served as afterthoughts to a piece of meat. Well chosen and properly cooked, vegetables make dishes in their own right that suffice for lunch or supper dishes when something light is required. Combined with pulses and dairy products, they can offer a complete alternative to a meat-based meal.

The recipes in this chapter vary from light salads made with perfectly ripe summer fruits and vegetables to their winter cousins that combine root vegetables and fungi. Mushrooms, wild and cultivated, appeared in great variety at the restaurant thanks to the research of several staff members, notably Nick Coiley who now owns a brilliant restaurant named after one – Agaric in Ashburton. When we cook a vegetable in a more elaborate dish, we aim to highlight particular flavours by adding complementary ingredients. You will see this in the recipe for Chicory and red onion tart Tatin, where the natural sweetness of the vegetables is accentuated by honey and orange superbly.

Much vegetarian cookery verges on the worthy, even today, so we wanted to include a variety of dishes which celebrate the best aspects of vegetables for their own sake, and which can be enjoyed by all.

Avocado and melon salad
with elderflower or tarragon dressing

At the restaurant we used to have trays of melons and avocados ripening in the boiler room – the demand for them from the kitchen meant that we had to work hard to keep up – and any that did not ripen evenly would have their ripest, most flavoursome parts used in sorbets or guacamole. Nothing ever went to waste. In the height of summer, a handful of ripe strawberries would make a nice addition to this salad.

Serves 4

method

Combine the oil, vinegar, sugar, salt and pepper in a blender. While it is running, gradually add the cream until the dressing is evenly mixed. Check the seasoning and adjust as necessary, then keep cool until required.

Halve and stone the avocados, then peel and slice and arrange the slices on plates. Repeat with the melon. Spoon over the dressing and garnish with the watercress and hazelnuts.

Note: To roast hazelnuts, place them on a baking tray in an oven preheated to 180C/Gas mark 5 and cook for 10-15 minutes until they are evenly browned. Allow them to cool and use a cloth to rub off the skins.

ingredients

2 large ripe Haas avocados
at room temperature

1 small ripe Galia melon
at room temperature

1 bunch watercress, washed and thick stems removed

20g roasted hazelnuts, skinned and chopped

For the dressing:

150ml groundnut oil

3 tbsp tarragon or elderflower vinegar

1 tsp sugar

Salt and freshly ground black pepper

150ml single cream

Artichoke gratin

This artichoke and potato gratin is a perfect accompaniment to winter meat or game dishes. The aromatic sweetness of the artichokes adds a real depth of flavour to the potatoes and cream.

Serves 6

METHOD

Layer the potato and artichoke in a gratin dish. Season each layer as you go and finish with a layer of potato. Pour on the cream until it is almost all covered. Bake in the oven at 190C/Gas mark 5 for about 45 minutes, or until the cream has reduced and is golden brown. During cooking the heat will often raise the vegetables so that they lift out of the liquid. Flatten them occasionally with a palette knife to ensure they are kept moist and cook evenly.

ingredients

450g old potatoes such as King Edward or Desiree, peeled and thinly sliced

225g Jerusalem artichokes, peeled, thinly sliced and blanched in boiling water for one minute

Salt and pepper

300ml single cream

Spinach salad

The creamy texture of spinach is balanced in this salad with the earthy sweetness of mushrooms and parmesan cheese.

Serves 2 for a main course

method

Pick over the spinach to remove any bruised leaves or tough stems.

Put the egg yolk, lemon juice, garlic, salt and pepper into a blender and whizz to combine. While the blender is running, pour in the olive oil very slowly until it is emulsified. Stir in the grated cheese. Put the spinach in a bowl and add about half the dressing and the sliced mushrooms. Toss the salad then arrange it on a plate and finish with croutons.

Any excess dressing can be stored in the fridge and makes a lovely sauce for warm new potatoes, or for dipping asparagus spears. The salad could also be finished with crispy bacon or duck skin, or boiled, peeled and quartered hens or quails eggs.

ingredients

175g washed raw spinach, baby leaves if possible

4 button mushrooms, wiped clean and thinly sliced

For the dressing:

1 egg yolk

½ tbsp lemon juice

½ clove garlic, peeled

Salt and freshly ground black pepper

115ml olive oil

15g freshly grated parmesan cheese

For the croutons:

2 slices of good bread cut into 1cm cubes and deep-fried or toasted with a little oil until crisp

Artichoke, mushroom and hazelnut salad

An excellent winter salad that balances earthy textures and flavours.

Serves 4 as a light starter

method

In a blender, mix together the oils, vinegar, salt and pepper to taste, then set aside. Slice the mushrooms thinly.

Bring a pan of water to a simmer, and place a steamer on top. Peel the artichokes and slice into fine sections on a mandolin. Steam until just cooked then set aside to cool. Add the mushrooms and half the hazelnuts and mix together.

Arrange the chicory and watercress on a plate. Dress the artichokes and mushrooms with the dressing and arrange on the salad. Finish with the rest of the hazelnuts and the chopped parsley.

Note: To roast hazelnuts, place them on a baking tray in an oven preheated to 180C/Gas mark 5 and cook for 10-15 minutes until they are evenly browned. Allow them to cool and use a cloth to rub off the skins.

ingredients

115g Jerusalem artichokes

115g button mushrooms

55g roasted hazelnuts, skinned and chopped

2 chicory spears, sliced into long pieces

Small bunch watercress, thick stems removed

Small bunch flat-leaf parsley, chopped

For the dressing:

150ml groundnut oil

30ml hazelnut oil

50ml white wine vinegar

Salt and freshly ground black pepper

Red onion and apricot confit

Mellow and sweet, this vegetable and fruit mixture is sharpened with a little vinegar to balance the flavours. This is nice as a relish for game or poultry dishes

Serves 6 as an accompaniment

method

Heat the oil in a pan until it is very hot and then fry the onions with the sugar so that they begin to caramelise. Add the thinly sliced apricots and orange peel. Season well and add the vinegar, then reduce the liquid until the mixture is thick.

ingredients

40ml light olive oil

450g red onions, peeled and thinly sliced

25g granulated sugar

175g apricots, thinly sliced

Peel of 1½ oranges shredded into juliennes

30ml red wine or cider vinegar

Mushroom tart

Crisp, buttery pastry and creamy mushrooms – delicious!

Serves 6

method

Melt the butter in a medium pan over a low to medium heat. Sauté the onions and garlic for about five minutes until they are soft but not coloured. Add the mushrooms and continue to cook, stirring, until the liquid evaporates and the mixture is almost dry. Season assertively with salt, pepper and a little nutmeg and put in the bottom of the pastry case. Mix together the egg yolks, cream and parsley and pour over the mushroom filling. Bake in the oven at 190C/Gas mark 5 for 20-30 minutes, or until the custard is just firm and a little brown on top. Allow the tart to cool a little in the tin before removing to a serving plate. Eat while still just warm.

ingredients

1 batch shortcrust pastry made with 300g plain flour and 150g unsalted butter (see page 113), blind baked in a 23cm flan tin, or in 6 individual tart cases

For the filling:

55g unsalted butter

1 large onion, peeled and finely chopped

2 cloves garlic, peeled and finely chopped

225g button mushrooms, wiped and coarsely chopped

3 egg yolks

300ml single cream

2 tbsp parsley, washed, tough stems removed, chopped

Salt, freshly ground black pepper and nutmeg

Chicory and red onion tart Tatin

This tart was developed to make a delicious, smart vegetarian main course – deep and rich in flavour. It makes a special first course too.

Serves 4 as a starter

method

First make the pastry. Combine the flour, ground rice and butter in a food processor until the mixture resembles breadcrumbs. Mix in the orange zest then gradually add the egg, pulsing the machine until it is all incorporated. Do not over-mix or the pastry will become tough. Wrap the ball of dough in cling film and put it in the fridge for at least 30 minutes.

To make the filling, melt the butter, honey and orange juice together in a pan and divide between four 15cm ovenproof metal gratin dishes or one 23cm skillet or cake tin. Arrange the onion and chicory in the dishes and put them on the heat until they start to caramelise and turn brown. Remove them from the heat and sprinkle them with the spices and a little seasoning. Cool the vegetables in their dishes until you are ready to finish the dish.

Roll out the pastry to a thickness of 5mm and cut into rounds that will fit on the rims of the dishes. Lay the pastry on top of the onions and chicory and press down lightly. Bake in the oven at 200C/Gas mark 6 for about 15 minutes or until the pastry is golden brown. Allow the tarts to cool slightly and then turn them out carefully onto warmed plates. Serve immediately.

ingredients

175g plain flour

55g ground rice

140g unsalted butter, cold

Zest of 1 orange, grated

1 egg, beaten

Salt and freshly ground black pepper

For the filling:

115g unsalted butter

1 tbsp English honey

1 tbsp orange juice

4 red onions, peeled and sliced in rounds

3 heads of chicory, sliced in rounds

Large pinch ground coriander

Pinch ground cinnamon

Salt and freshly ground black pepper

Spinach and watercress Pithivier

Crisp buttery pastry and a light nutty spinach filling make a super combination for this dish, which can be used either as a summer lunch or a picnic dish.

Serves 8 as a starter or 4 as a main course

method

Put the butter, almonds, flour, spinach, watercress, eggs and salt and pepper into a food processor and mix well. Cut the puff pastry in half and roll each piece into a circle 15-18cm diameter and a thickness of 2-3mm. Roll the second piece a little larger so that it will cover the first with the filling on top.

Line a baking tray with a sheet of non-stick baking paper and place the smaller sheet of pastry on the paper. Spread the filling over the pastry, leaving a border of about 2cm around the edge to brush with the beaten egg. Place the second piece on top and crimp the edges to seal them well, trimming any surplus pastry. Take a sharp knife and score the top of the Pithivier to resemble a spinning Catherine wheel, (see picture) then bake in an oven preheated to 220C/Gas mark 7 for about 20-25 minutes until it is risen and well browned.

ingredients

85g butter, softened

55g ground almonds

40g plain flour

115g spinach, washed and dried with the stems removed

25g watercress

2 eggs

350g home-made or all-butter puff pastry (see page 114)

1 egg, beaten, to glaze

Salt and freshly ground black pepper

Lemon/lime chutney

This chutney has the sharpest tang, and is excellent when served with cold poultry or game. Use lemons and limes in any proportion – whatever is available!

Makes 8-10 jars

method

Slice the lemons and limes and remove the pips. Put into a bowl with the sliced onions, vinegar and salt, and with the spices tied in a small square of muslin, and leave overnight.

The next day, preheat the oven to 120C/Gas mark 1 and put a few clean jam jars inside to sterilise them. Place the jar lids in a pan of water and boil for five minutes, then drain on kitchen paper.

Place all the ingredients but the sugar in a large stainless steel pan. Bring to a simmer over a high heat then reduce the heat and cook gently for about 90 minutes, or until the citrus peel is softened and tender. Remove the spices. Add the sugar and stir until dissolved. Increase the heat and boil fast for 20 minutes until the mixture is reduced and thickened to your liking. Divide between the jars and seal either with plastic lids or greaseproof paper and cellophane.

Keep for a couple of months in a dark place to mature before using.

ingredients

1.8kg unwaxed or organic lemons/ limes

900g onions, peeled and thinly sliced

1.2 litres white wine vinegar

25g salt

25g allspice

15g cardamom

15g coriander

115g fresh ginger, peeled and finely chopped

55g fresh chillies, deseeded and finely chopped

1.3kg granulated sugar

Guacamole

This lovely mixture is very adaptable, both as an accompaniment to shellfish and as a dip. It can also be used in place of mayonnaise in sandwiches with smoked chicken and bacon. Mix and use the guacamole immediately so it does not discolour.

Serves 4

method

Gently mix together all the ingredients and check the seasoning. Serve immediately.

ingredients

175g peeled, deseeded and diced tomatoes

2 large ripe Haas avocados, peeled, stoned and diced

1 shallot, chopped, blanched for one minute in boiling water, refreshed in cold water and drained

½ clove garlic, peeled and finely chopped

½ red chilli, deseeded and very finely chopped

85ml extra virgin olive oil

Zest and juice of 1 lime

Fresh parsley, chopped, to taste

Fresh coriander, chopped, to taste

Salt and pepper

Marinated aubergines
in honey and vinegar

This aromatic, smoky salad is best made a day before you intend to eat it to let the flavours amalgamate.

Serves 4 as a side dish to grilled meats or game

method

Slice the aubergine into discs about 5mm thick and season each slice on both sides. Heat a little oil in a frying pan over a medium high heat and fry a few slices until brown on both sides. Place the slices in a flat serving dish as you go and continue until they are all browned, adding a little more oil for each batch.

Put the oil, vinegar, honey and thyme into a pan and bring to a boil, then pour it over the aubergine. Leave for 24 hours to marinate. Before serving shred the basil and scatter it over the top.

ingredients

2 medium aubergines (about 700g)
Light olive oil for frying
Salt and freshly ground black pepper

For the dressing:
125ml extra virgin olive oil
3 tbsp white wine vinegar
1 tbsp liquid honey
1 sprig of fresh thyme
4 basil leaves

Grilled marinated vegetables

We are so much more conscious of the role of vegetables in their own right today. This mixture can be eaten on its own or on the side of grilled goats cheese or grilled meats.

Serves 4 as an accompaniment

method

Slice the aubergine and the courgette into discs about 5mm thick; peel and cut the red onion into thick slices; peel and slice the garlic; Deseed and quarter the peppers. Peel them by either grilling or using a blow torch to blister and char the skins and then remove. Brush everything with olive oil and season lightly with salt.

Grill all the vegetables, turning them as they brown, or cook on a low barbecue. Alternatively bake them in the oven at 170C/Gas mark 3 for about 40 minutes, with the addition of two heads of garlic, trimmed and halved. When they are all browned evenly, layer them in a serving dish.

Mix together the vinegar, olive oil and herbs with a little salt and pepper, and pour over the vegetables while they are still warm. Leave to marinate for 24 hours. They can be served at room temperature or reheated with a main course.

ingredients

1 medium aubergine (about 350g)

1 courgette

2 red onions, thickly sliced

1 red pepper

1 yellow pepper

2 cloves garlic

Olive oil for brushing

For the dressing:

Small bunch each of thyme, basil, marjoram and parsley, all finely chopped

30ml vinegar

125ml extra virgin olive oil

Red pepper soufflé Suissesse

A flavourful, light mixture that is savoury yet sweet – the perfect lunch or supper dish.

Serves 4

method

Dice the peeled and deseeded pepper, put half in a pan with the milk and bring almost to the boil. Transfer to a blender and purée until smooth. Melt the butter in a medium saucepan over a medium heat and sweat the remaining peppers with the garlic until they soften and become tender. Add the flour and stir to combine thoroughly, then add the parmesan and seasoning and cook a little longer until the cheese melts. Remove the pan from the heat, add the milk mixture and chopped parsley and beat it well until there are no lumps. Leave to cool slightly.

When the mixture has cooled a little, add the egg yolks and beat again. Whisk the egg whites until stiff and fold into the mixture. Butter four dariole moulds (tall metal soufflé dishes) and divide the mixture between them. Place the moulds in a deep tray with about 1cm of water in the bottom and cook in the oven for 20 minutes at 200C/Gas mark 6 until firm to the touch.

When the soufflés are cool, turn them out into individual ovenproof dishes and pour over the double cream. Sprinkle with a little extra parmesan and bake in a hot oven (220C/Gas mark 7) for about six minutes until well risen and browned. For a more substantial dish, turn the soufflés out onto a bed of sweated mushrooms or leeks before baking them again.

ingredients

175g red peppers, peeled and deseeded (Peel them by either grilling or using a blow torch to blister and char the skins and then remove)

150ml milk

25g unsalted butter

½ clove garlic, peeled and chopped

25g plain flour

1 tbsp fresh parmesan, finely grated, plus an additional 2 tbsp for baking

2 tbsp chopped parsley

2 eggs, separated

150ml double cream

Salt and freshly ground black pepper

Parsnip and apple bake

A lovely accompaniment to roast game or pork.

Serves 4

method

Cut the parsnips into even chunks and boil in lightly salted water. When tender, drain them and purée in a processor with about half the butter. Season with a little salt and pepper to taste. Peel and slice the apples and mix with the lemon juice.

Layer the apple and parsnip purée in a dish, finishing with the apple. Dot with the rest of the butter and sprinkle with the sugar. Bake for about 30 minutes in a moderate oven (180C/Gas mark 4) until the apple is tender.

ingredients

225g parsnips, peeled and cored

55g unsalted butter

225g cooking apples

Juice of ½ lemon

15g granulated sugar

Salt and freshly ground black pepper

Apple, celeriac and horseradish salad

Earthy and sweet, this salad makes an excellent accompaniment to smoked fish such as eel or salmon. Serve them with malted bread and a glass of pinot gris or Gewürztraminer for a perfect lunch.

Serves 4 as an accompaniment

method

Mix the first six ingredients together, taking care not to break up the pieces of celeriac and apple.

Then season with salt and pepper, add the lemon juice and serve immediately.

ingredients

55g celeriac, peeled and julienned, blanched for one minute in boiling water, then refreshed

1 Cox's apple, sliced or cut into strips

1 tbsp mayonnaise

1 tbsp double cream

Bunch chives or flat-leaf parsley, chopped

1 tbsp fresh horseradish, finely grated

Lemon juice to taste

Salt and freshly ground black pepper

Spiced apple chutney

Both at home and in the restaurant, chutney making happened in autumn, though in quite different quantities! Lovely with cheese and pork pies, this is worth making in quantity for a year-round supply.

Makes 6-8 jars

method

Sprinkle the apples with the salt and set aside. Preheat the oven to 120C/Gas mark 1 and put a few clean jam jars inside to sterilise them. Place the jar lids in a pan of water and boil for five minutes, then drain on kitchen paper.

Heat the oil in a large stainless steel pan over a medium heat, add the ginger and garlic and fry gently until just brown. Add the mustard seeds, fenugreek, peppercorns, cumin, chillies, turmeric and chilli powder and fry for a few minutes, stirring well. Add the apples, vinegar and sugar and continue to stir over a low heat for about 30 minutes, till the chutney has thickened and the apples are soft and pulpy. Divide between the jars and seal either with plastic lids or greaseproof paper and cellophane.

Keep for a couple of months in a dark place to mature before using.

ingredients

900g cooking apples, peeled and sliced into small chunks

2 tsp salt

150ml vegetable oil

1 inch piece of ginger, peeled and grated

1 head of garlic, peeled and finely chopped

2 tbsp white mustard seeds

1 tsp fenugreek seeds, soaked in water for 30 minutes then drained

15 black peppercorns

2 tsp ground cumin

4 fresh chillies, deseeded and chopped

1 tsp turmeric

1 tsp chilli powder

150ml cider vinegar

115g granulated or light brown sugar

Quince cheese

Makes 3-4 jars

method

Wash quinces. Put into a casserole dish or roasting tin, cover closely with tinfoil and cook in a cool oven, 150C/300F/Gas mark 2, for about 2 to 3 hours or until really tender. Remove the quinces and puree through a 'mouli au legumes' or food processor whilst still hot. If using the latter it will also need passing through a fine sieve to remove debris. Weigh the puree and to each 450g of puree, add 350g sugar. Place the mixture in a large saucepan over a medium heat and stir to dissolve the sugar. When it is dissolved, increase the heat to high and cook, stirring constantly with a wooden spoon to prevent burning. The mixture is ready when the wooden spoon passed through the centre shows the base of the pan.

Pour into sterilized jars and seal. Small straight sided jars for ease of turning out are useful containers if you want to serve the quince cheese with a cheese course.

ingredients

1.3 kg quince

granulated sugar – see method

Red cabbage with apple and orange

Braised red cabbage is one of the joys of winter – good enough to eat on its own with brown bread and butter for lunch, and an excellent accompaniment to roast poultry, pork and game. The bacon is an optional addition.

Serves 4-6 as an accompaniment

method

Quarter the cabbage, remove and discard the white core and shred the purple leaves. Put into a bowl with the onion, apple and seasoning.

Put the sunflower oil and the bacon or dripping (if using) into a heavy casserole over a medium heat and melt to sizzle. Add the contents of the bowl and cook on the stove until the vegetables begin to wilt, which will take about five minutes. Add the port, vinegar, sugar and orange zest and stir well to combine. Cover and cook gently, stirring occasionally, for about an hour or until the cabbage is really tender. If at any point the cabbage seems dry or begins to stick to the pan, add a splash of water and continue to cook until it is tender. Taste before serving, as the seasoning may need adjusting.

ingredients

1 small red cabbage (about 800g)

1 onion, peeled and thinly sliced

2 cooking apples, peeled and sliced (about 600g)

2 tbsp sunflower oil

6 rashers bacon, cut into strips, or a little pork or duck dripping (optional)

2 tbsp port

2 tbsp red wine or cider vinegar

2 tbsp granulated or light brown sugar

Zest of 1 orange, grated

Salt and freshly ground black pepper

Pasta and rice

It would be possible to fill many books with traditional recipes for pasta, so this chapter contains a selection of the best and simplest dishes. It's easy to learn to make good pasta at home, and to experiment pairing pastas with sauces, with very little outlay. A home pasta machine will give excellent results and you will be surprised how inexpensive good quality pasta is to make. Half a kilo of flour will make several servings of spaghetti or ribbon noodles, and drying the pasta or freezing it in single portions will allow you to cook an easy meal in a matter of minutes at a later date.

Many of us tend to eat less solid protein today. Pasta is increasingly popular because it can be paired with such a great variety of ingredients, so it's not surprising that many cuisines from around the world use noodles in one form or another. To reflect this, you will find sauces here from both Italy and the Far East.

Rice, too, is incredibly versatile and available in many forms. In this chapter you will find recipes for risotto as well as sushi and cooked pilafs.

Pasta

This basic pasta dough can be varied by adding herbs and other flavourings to suit your sauce. At the restaurant we made pasta almost on a daily basis, such was its popularity and versatility. If you make a batch at home, you can freeze portions of freshly cut noodles on a tray, ready to drop into boiling water – they will cook from frozen in a matter of minutes.

Makes 8 large portions

method

Put all the ingredients except the water into a food processor and mix well. If necessary add water until the crumbs begin to form larger nuggets of pasta which you can bring together into a supple dough with your fingers. Wrap the dough in cling film and chill for at least half an hour.

If you have a pasta machine, cut the dough into eight pieces and roll each out at the thickest setting several times. Fold the dough in half between each rolling (this will knead the dough and making it smooth and even). Once you have rolled all the pieces five or six times, continue rolling the dough through thinner and thinner settings until you have rolled all the sheets to your desired thickness, usually the thinnest.

If you do not have a pasta machine, use a rolling pin to roll out the dough on a lightly floured surface to a thickness through which you can read a sheet of newspaper.

At this stage, you can cut the sheets to make any type of pasta you like, or save them whole, layered between cling film, for making ravioli or lasagne. Alternatively, cut into noodles and freeze for up to one month.

To cook, add the pasta to boiling salted water, bring back to the boil and drain. Put into a bowl and add your sauce, or return to the pan and dress with the sauce before serving.

This quantity makes enough pasta for eight healthy appetites.

VARIATIONS

To make flavoured pasta, simply add any one of the following to 550g flour:

1) 55g roasted hazelnuts, finely ground
2) 30ml green peppercorns in brine, drained and finely chopped
3) 55g basil, dill or parsley, finely chopped
4) 55g lobster coral
5) 50ml squid ink
6) 115g sorrel or spinach, chopped
7) 2 tsp tomato purée
8) replace half the pasta flour with an equal quantity of buckwheat flour

ingredients

550g pasta flour (type 00)
4 whole eggs
2 egg yolks
1 pinch salt
Water (if needed)

Stir fried vegetables
with noodles, chilli and soy sauce

Spicy and light, this vegetable and noodle recipe is a simple, all-in-one dish.

Serves 4 as a starter or 2 as a main course

method

Slice all the vegetables very thinly. Heat a wok or a large deep frying pan over a high heat. Add the oils, onion, garlic, ginger, peppers, baby corn, chilli and bean sprouts. Keep moving the wok and stirring the vegetables so nothing sticks and everything cooks evenly. Add the oyster mushrooms, then the noodles. Finally add the liquids and bring the mixture to a boil.

Check the seasoning, add a pinch of sugar and serve immediately.

ingredients

1 tsp sesame oil

1 tbsp groundnut oil

1 small onion peeled

1 clove of garlic, peeled

25g fresh ginger, peeled and finely grated

1 small yellow pepper

1 small red pepper

1 baby corn

1 small red chilli

55g bean sprouts

115g oyster mushrooms, wiped

225g egg noodles, cooked and drained

1 tsp soy sauce

1 splash Thai fish sauce (optional)

150ml vegetable stock (see page 33)

1 pinch palm sugar or demerara

Salt and freshly ground black pepper

Mushroom sauce
for pasta

This light sauce is perfect for an autumn lunch or supper dish. You can use any mushrooms you like.

Serves 4

method

In a medium saucepan, melt the butter over a medium heat. Add the garlic, onion and half the mushrooms and cook together for five minutes with a pinch of salt, until the vegetables are softened and cooked. Add the milk, transfer to a blender and purée. Return to the pan with the remaining mushrooms and cook briefly. Season to taste and serve with hazelnut pasta or a pasta of your choice.

ingredients

25g unsalted butter

1 clove garlic, peeled and finely chopped

115g onion, peeled and finely chopped

330g mushrooms, wiped and finely sliced

300ml milk

Salt and freshly ground black pepper

Leek and mushroom sauce
for pasta

A lovely autumnal mixture, light and fragrant.

Serves 4

method

In a medium saucepan, melt half the butter over a low heat and add the leeks and garlic. Cook, stirring occasionally until the leeks begin to release their juices, then raise the heat to evaporate the liquid. Be careful not to brown the leeks. Add the milk and cream, and bring the pan to the boil over a medium to high heat. Cook, stirring occasionally for five minutes until the leeks are tender. Purée the mixture in a liquidizer and keep to one side while you cook the mushrooms.

Heat the remaining butter in a frying pan over a high heat and add the mushrooms with a pinch of salt and pepper. Stir the pan until the mushrooms begin to brown at the edges, then add the contents of the blender and reduce the heat to a low simmer until the sauce has amalgamated. Taste for seasoning, adding a little nutmeg to taste. Serve immediately over freshly cooked pasta.

ingredients

25g unsalted butter

225g leeks, cleaned and sliced

1 clove garlic, peeled and sliced

150ml milk

150ml single cream

225g mushrooms, wiped and finely sliced

Salt, freshly ground black pepper and nutmeg

Tomatoes, black olives and basil
with pasta

The success of this raw sauce relies on using only the very tastiest ripe tomatoes and best olive oil.

Serves 4

method

Mix all the ingredients in a large bowl, add 400g hot, freshly cooked pasta and toss together to combine.

ingredients

230g tomatoes, peeled and diced (see method for pesto on page 52)

24 black olives, stoned and chopped

1 small bunch fresh basil leaves, shredded

100ml best olive oil

Salt and black pepper to taste

Pesto

Simply one of the very best flavour combinations.

Serves 4

method

First, peel the tomatoes. Cut a light cross on the base of each fruit and place in a medium bowl. Pour over enough boiling water to cover the tomatoes and leave for one minute. Then drain off the hot water and replace with cold. When the tomatoes are cool, drain them and peel off the skin. Cut the tomatoes in half and discard the seeds.

Put all the ingredients except the olive oil in a food processor. Switch on and gradually add the oil to make a thickish paste. Put on top of hot pasta and mix gently.

The pesto will keep for one week in the fridge if covered with a good layer of oil.

ingredients

2 ripe tomatoes

55g fresh basil leaves

55g pine kernels, lightly toasted

2 cloves garlic, peeled

55g parmesan cheese, grated

Salt and freshly ground black pepper

Olive oil

Scallop and mussel sauce
for pasta

Sweet and delicious, this sauce goes well with fresh pasta for a tasty lunch.

Serves 4 as a starter

method

Place a medium saucepan over a medium heat and add the olive oil. Add the onion and garlic and a pinch of salt. Cook for three or four minutes until the onions begin to soften. Add the tomatoes and bring to a simmer over a low heat.

Meanwhile place another medium or large saucepan over a high heat and add the mussels and 100ml white wine. Place the lid on the pan and allow the mussels to open, which will take only one or two minutes. As soon as they have opened, remove from the heat and drain, adding the strained liquid to the sauce. Pick the mussels out of their shells and reserve, discarding the shells.

Once the sauce has cooked for five minutes or so, and the pieces of tomato have broken down, the dish can be brought together. If you are serving this sauce with pasta, make sure the pasta is almost ready before you finish the sauce so that the shellfish does not overcook.

Chop the scallops into pea-sized pieces and cut the mussels in half. Chop the herbs finely and add to the sauce with the shellfish. Simmer for one minute, then remove from the heat and let it sit for a further minute. Check the seasoning and add a little lemon juice. Serve immediately.

ingredients

4 tbsp extra virgin olive oil

2 medium onions, peeled and finely chopped

3 cloves garlic, peeled and finely chopped

280g fresh ripe tomatoes, peeled and chopped (see method for pesto on page 52)

18 mussels, cleaned and de-bearded

100ml white wine

6 scallops, cleaned

1 small bunch parsley or basil

Salt and freshly ground black pepper

Lemon juice to taste

Coriander and coconut dressing

Serves 4

method

Put all the ingredients except the oil in a food processor and mix to a thick paste. Add oil to slacken the dressing to a consistency that will just hold its shape. This is excellent with Chinese noodles served alongside steamed fish or chicken.

ingredients

100g fresh coriander

60g creamed coconut, grated

1 clove garlic, peeled and sliced

1 inch piece fresh ginger, peeled and finely grated

1-2 green chillies, seeded and chopped

Grated rind and juice of 2 limes

Salt to taste

Olive oil or peanut oil

Spiced Sichuan noodles

Here, the pork balls are fried until brown and crispy then served on a delicious mixture of spiced vegetables and noodles.

Serves 4

method

Combine the pork, soy sauce and ½ tsp salt in a small bowl and mix well. Shape the pork into small balls and lay them out on a tray.

Add the peanut oil to a wok or frying pan to a depth of about 1cm and turn up the heat. When the oil is hot, fry the pork balls until they are a deep brown all over and cooked through. Check by cutting one in half, if the middle is still pink, cook for a minute longer, then retest. When the pork balls are cooked, drain them on kitchen paper to absorb any excess oil.

Discard most of the oil, leaving about 2 tbsp in the wok or frying pan. Place over a high heat and add the ginger, spring onions and garlic. Stir fry for 30 seconds, then add the sesame paste, soy, chilli oil and a good pinch of salt, keeping everything moving over the heat. Then add the chicken stock and simmer for four minutes until you have a light, aromatic sauce.

Meanwhile bring a large pot of water to the boil and cook the noodles according to the instructions on the packet. Drain them well, put in a deep serving bowl and add the sauce. Garnish with the fried pork balls and Sichuan peppercorns.

ingredients

225g minced pork

1 tbsp dark soy sauce

½ tsp salt

225ml peanut oil

50g fresh ginger, peeled and finely grated

5 tbsp finely chopped spring onions

6 cloves garlic, peeled and finely chopped

2 tbsp sesame paste or peanut butter

2 tbsp dark soy sauce

2 tbsp chilli oil

2 tsp salt

225ml chicken stock (see page 31)

350g dry Chinese egg noodles

1 tbsp Sichuan peppercorns, roasted and ground, to serve

Lemon, chicken and gruyère sauce for pasta

A rich, aromatic mixture that is perfect for lunch on a chilly day.

Serves 2

method

Place the wine in a medium saucepan over a medium heat. Add the finely grated lemon zest and simmer for two minutes. Add the chicken strips and a little salt and pepper, and heat through. Reduce the heat to low and add the soured cream or crème fraîche, then the gruyère, stirring until the sauce is amalgamated and the cheese has melted. Serve immediately over freshly cooked parsley noodles or a pasta of your choice.

ingredients

100ml light, medium dry white wine

Zest of 1 lemon, finely grated

125g cooked chicken, cut into strips

150g soured cream or full fat crème fraîche

85g gruyère cheese, grated

Salt and freshly ground black pepper

Sushi

Our version of sushi, made with the finest British salmon, is delicious. Use wild salmon if you can be sure it has been caught sustainably, alternatively use high-welfare farmed salmon such as that from Loch Duart or other suppliers recommended by the RSPCA (see back of book).

Makes 4 rolls (enough for 30-40 pieces)

method

Place a medium saucepan over a high heat, add the water and bring to a boil. Add the rice and simmer over a low to medium heat until tender. Drain through a sieve and stir in the dill and a large pinch of salt. Spread the rice out on a clean tray or a plate to cool.

Heat a little water in a medium pan over a high heat and add the spring onion tops. Cook, stirring for one minute until they are limp, then drain and cool. Check the salmon for bones and remove any with tweezers. Cut the salmon into long strips, place in a shallow dish and pour over the lime juice. Leave to cool in the fridge for ten minutes.

Mix together the ingredients for the brushing sauce in a bowl, then lay the nori sheets out on cling film and brush with the liquid. Divide the rice between the sheets and spread out evenly. Spread the spring onions out along the front edge of the nori sheets on top of the rice, and divide the salmon between the four sheets on top of the spring onions.

Using the cling film to help you, lift each sheet in turn and roll away from you so that the salmon is at the centre of the roll. Be careful not to trap the cling film in the roll as you work. Roll the sheets up firmly then wrap each roll in cling film, squeezing tightly. Chill for up to four hours.

When ready to eat, unwrap each roll and slice into 2cm slices. Serve with wasabi, soy sauce and pickled ginger.

ingredients

600ml water

1 large pinch salt

200ml uncooked sushi rice

2 tbsp chopped fresh dill

4 spring onions (green tops only)

140g boneless salmon fillet, skinned

Juice of 1 lime

4 nori sheets

For the brushing sauce:

50ml soy sauce

1 inch piece root ginger, peeled and finely grated

Zest of 1 lime, finely grated

2 tsp rice wine or dry sherry

1 splash Thai fish sauce

Grated horseradish (optional)

Pepper

Wasabi paste, pickled ginger and soy sauce to serve

Coconut rice

An aromatic, rich pilaf to serve with a simple fish or poultry dish.

Serves 4 as an accompaniment

method

Heat the butter in a medium pan over a low to medium heat. Add the garlic and ginger and cook, stirring for two minutes. Add the rice and fry gently, stirring for another minute or two.

Place the creamed coconut in a small pan and pour over the boiling stock or water, stirring to dissolve, and add the lemon juice. Pour over the rice and add a little salt, pepper and turmeric. Turn the heat to low and cover the pan. Cook for 12-15 minutes, removing from the heat when all the liquid has been absorbed. It could also be cooked in the oven: once the stock or water has been added, simply cover the pan and pop it into a low oven (140C/Gas mark 1) for 15 minutes. To serve, simply stir in the cream and check the seasoning.

ingredients

25g unsalted butter

1 small clove garlic, peeled and finely chopped

1 small piece fresh ginger, peeled and grated

115g basmati rice

40g creamed coconut

150ml chicken stock (see page 31) or boiling water

Juice of ½ lemon

Salt and freshly ground black pepper

1 pinch turmeric

50ml single cream

Saffron pilaf

A combination of aromatic vegetables and rice that is lovely served with roast or grilled meat and poultry.

Serves 4

method

Preheat the oven to 140C/Gas mark 1.

Heat the butter in an ovenproof pan or casserole dish over a medium heat. Add the onion, garlic and pepper and fry gently for five minutes, until the vegetables are softened and beginning to colour. Add the rice and stir to combine. Add the saffron and water or stock and bring to the boil, then add a pinch of salt and cover the dish.

Place in the oven for 12-15 minutes or until the rice is tender. Fluff up the rice with a large fork and check the seasoning. Serve with roast meats.

ingredients

55g unsalted butter

1 large onion, peeled and finely chopped

1 clove garlic, peeled and finely chopped

1 red pepper, halved, seeded and finely sliced

225g basmati rice, well washed and drained

1 pinch saffron, pounded

300ml chicken stock (see page 31) or water

Salt and freshly ground black pepper

Lobster risotto

You only need a little shellfish for this risotto, making it quite economical. If you have access to shells regularly, freeze them until you have enough to make the stock.

Serves 4 as a starter

method

Place a pan on a medium heat and add the butter and olive oil. When the butter is sizzling, add the onion and cook, stirring for three or four minutes. Then add the fennel and a little salt and pepper and cook for another three minutes or so until soft.

Add the rice and stir for a couple of minutes until thoroughly coated with the vegetables and oil. Add the wine and bring the mixture to a simmer. Reduce until all the wine has been absorbed. Add half the stock and a pinch of saffron then bring back to the boil. Once boiling, remove from the heat. At this point the risotto base can be kept in the fridge until needed or finished off straight away.

To finish, preheat the oven to 150C/Gas mark 2. Add the remaining stock and bring to the boil, mixing gently with a fork, then put into a cool oven for five minutes. Add the lobster meat (and the coral if you have any) and mix in gently. Taste for seasoning and return the pan to the oven for another five minutes. Remove the risotto from the oven and fork through before serving. The mixture should be just firm enough to hold its shape in a soft yielding mass. If it's too firm, add a splash of stock or water to loosen it.

ingredients

25g unsalted butter

30ml light olive oil

1 medium onion, peeled and chopped

1 head fennel, washed well and finely chopped

225g risotto rice

750ml shellfish stock (see page 32)

150ml white wine

1 pinch saffron

225g cooked lobster meat, including the coral if there is any

Salt and pepper

Mushroom risotto

A complete dish in itself, this risotto combines the delicate flavours of rice, stock and mushrooms to produce a dish that is far greater than the sum of its parts.

Serves 4

method

Heat the stock in a saucepan over a medium heat. Bring it to a gentle simmer then reduce the heat to low.

Heat the butter and oil in a separate pan over a medium heat. Add the finely chopped onion and cook, stirring for two or three minutes. Add a pinch of salt and pepper and the finely chopped garlic, and cook for another two or three minutes until soft. Add the rice and stir to combine. Add the red wine and simmer until all the wine has been absorbed.

Add about half the stock, the chopped thyme and the bay leaf, and raise the heat. Cook over a medium heat, stirring until the rice has absorbed nearly all the liquid. Add more stock, a ladleful at a time, stirring constantly, and allowing the rice to absorb the liquid between ladles. Continue until the rice is cooked and the stock has been almost all absorbed. You may need a little more or less stock, depending on the type of rice you have used. Add the mushrooms and allow them to cook through in the hot rice. Their liquid will be absorbed by the rice and will delicately flavour the risotto. Season to taste with additional salt and pepper. Stir through the final addition of butter and parmesan. Serve immediately.

ingredients

750ml chicken stock (see page 31) or vegetable stock (see page 33)

25g unsalted butter

1 tbsp olive oil

1 medium onion, peeled and finely chopped

1 small clove garlic, peeled and finely chopped

225g risotto rice

150ml red wine

2 tsp fresh thyme, chopped

1 bay leaf

225g mushrooms, wiped and sliced finely

Salt and freshly ground black pepper

40g unsalted butter and 40g finely grated parmesan to serve

Rice croquettes

It is worth making extra risotto just for this dish.

Using cold leftover risotto, take a tablespoonful and flatten in the palm of your hand. Squash in a piece of mozzarella, gruyère or blue cheese, and roll the cold rice into a ball around the cheese. Chill the croquettes, then coat them in egg and roll them in breadcrumbs. Deep fry and serve with tomato sauce.

Fish and shellfish

As an island nation, we are surprisingly conservative in our choice of fish. Yet our seas produce a huge variety of delicious species, and chefs and cooks are increasingly aware of issues surrounding sustainability. When you are selecting fish to cook, look for indications that they have been caught or farmed sustainably. The Marine Stewardship Council monitors fishing activity around the world and only puts its stamp of approval on fisheries that have passed its independent scrutiny. For farmed fish, look to the RSPCA Freedom Food Award to tell you that the fish have been responsibly cared for with minimal environmental impact.

At the restaurant, we were blessed with many small suppliers fishing from local day boats. These tended to be single-handed operations that were weather dependent, so we often had to rely on the fishmonger in the winter months who would bring in fish from further away. The selection of recipes in this chapter reflects the wide range of our supply, but you should feel that you can substitute one fish for another – white fish in particular are often interchangeable. Oily fish, such as mackerel and herring are best grilled simply with lemon and butter, or served with a spiced sauce such as the Five Willow Sauce that you will find in this chapter.

Shellfish, particularly crab, lobster and scallops are highly valued and remain popular, if premium choices, and you will find several recipes in this book for using these for special occasions. We were lucky to be able to buy fresh live prawns from Robert Dart, a local fisherman who supplied us for many years. The cold waters around our islands cause shellfish to grow slowly, allowing them to develop fine, rich flavours that are unequalled anywhere in the world.

Some people fear fish cookery, and it's true that fish can easily be overcooked. If you are new to cooking, experiment with the less expensive fish first – coley, pollock and mackerel are all easily sourced and well worth buying. Once you have some confidence, move on to the premium fish and make the most of this wonderful resource.

Fish bourride

This rich fish stew can be made with a variety of fish, but non-oily, white fish is best. Pollock, coley, dogfish or whiting would all make an inexpensive stew, while monkfish or turbot would be delicious for a special occasion.

Serves 4 as a main course

method

Preheat the oven to 150 C/Gas mark 2.

Trim the green from the leeks, leaving just the white parts – you should have about 225g left – and slice them. Heat the oil in a large flameproof casserole over a medium heat and gently sauté the leeks, garlic and fennel for five minutes. Add the tomatoes, white wine, lemon juice, saffron, thyme, marjoram, bay leaf and a little salt and pepper and cook gently for ten minutes, uncovered. Cut the fish into neat, equal-sized pieces and add to the pan. Cover with a tightly fitting lid and bake in the oven for about five minutes or until the fish is tender. Carefully lift the fish from the pan and place on a heated serving dish to keep warm. Stir the aioli into the sauce and return to the stove, stirring gently to thicken the sauce, being careful not to boil, which would curdle the eggs in the mayonnaise. Season to taste and remove from the heat. Extract the bay leaf and pour the sauce over the fish. Chop the parsley and sprinkle over the stew, along with the croutons.

To make croutons:

Lightly oil a baking tray and lay out some thinly cut slices of baguette. Bake in a warm oven (180C/Gas mark 4) until the bread is lightly toasted and has absorbed the oil, which will take approximately 15 minutes. You could also make small round croutons successfully using bagels. When sliced and roasted with a little oil the small circles are ideal for soups and dips.

ingredients

350g leeks, well washed and drained

3 tbsp olive oil

2 cloves garlic, peeled and finely chopped

225g fennel, washed and sliced

200g canned tomatoes, drained and chopped

150ml white wine

Lemon juice to taste

¼ tsp saffron strands

2 sprigs thyme

2 sprigs marjoram

1 bay leaf

900g fish, filleted and pin boned

Salt

Freshly ground black pepper

4 tbsp aioli (garlic mayonnaise, see below)

1 small bunch fresh parsley washed and dried

Croutons baked in olive oil

Aioli (garlic mayonnaise)

Note: use a mild olive oil for this recipe. Too strong a flavour from the oil masks the garlic and anything you are serving the mayonnaise with. Three parts sunflower oil to one part extra virgin oil can be used if you do not have any mild oil.

method

Place the garlic, salt and lemon juice in the jug of a liquidizer or small blender. Purée well, then add the yolks. Purée again, and carefully add the oil in small additions, allowing the machine to run all the time. As you add the oil, you will notice that the sauce thickens considerably. If it should become so thick that it does not flow in the machine, add a little water and continue. When all the oil is added, check the seasoning, and store in the fridge for up to 3 days, tightly covered.

ingredients

3 cloves fresh garlic, peeled

¼ tsp salt

1 tbsp lemon juice

2 egg yolks

250 ml olive oil (see note on page 61)

Black pepper to taste

Grilled turbot
with fennel and black olive sauce

Turbot is one of the finest fishes you will come across – its firm and delicious flesh is a real treat. The subtle flavours of the olive and fennel sauce complement it perfectly.

Serves 4

method

Heat 2 tbsp olive oil in a medium pan over a low to medium heat. Sauté the shallot, garlic, fennel and olives until they soften but do not allow them to colour. This will take about five minutes. Cover with the stock or water and the sherry, simmer gently for about 45 minutes and then set aside to cool for a further five minutes. Carefully transfer the contents of the pan to a food processor and blend until smooth, gradually adding the olive oil. Season the sauce to taste, pass it through a fine sieve and then keep it just warm in a bowl over a pan of hot but not boiling water.

When you are ready to cook the fish, preheat the grill and place the shelf about 10cm underneath the element. Season the turbot with salt and pepper and put it onto a baking tray. Add a little lemon juice and a dribble of olive oil. Place under the hot grill for about five minutes, then turn the fish and grill the other side for a further five minutes. The fish is cooked when you can just ease the flakes apart with a fork. Serve with the black olive sauce and lemon wedges.

ingredients

A little olive oil

1 shallot, peeled and chopped

1 clove of garlic, peeled and chopped

175g fennel, chopped

6 black olives, stones removed

200ml fish stock or water (see page 32

125ml fino sherry

4 × 175g turbot steaks

100ml extra virgin olive oil for finishing the sauce

Lemon juice to taste

Salt and pepper

Herb hollandaise
method

Put the lemon juice, egg and seasoning into a blender. Heat the butter until just starting to froth. Start the blender and gradually pour in the hot butter. When all the butter has been amalgamated, add the herbs and continue to blend until they are puréed finely. Pour the hollandaise back into the butter pan and continue to stir constantly over a very low heat until the sauce is thick and glossy, making sure not to let it curdle. If it shows signs of curdling (when the egg begins to scramble and form small lumps) pour it immediately through a sieve into a cold bowl. Check the seasoning, add any juices from the fish and stir well.

ingredients

225g unsalted butter

2 tbsp soft fresh herbs, such as tarragon, chervil, chives and parsley, washed and chopped

Juice of ½ lemon

1 egg

Salt and cayenne pepper

Monkfish 'au poivre'

This impressive dish is rich and flavoursome and needs little accompaniment other than some steamed green beans or perhaps a herb salad lightly dressed with oil and lemon.

Serves 4 as a starter

method

Mix together the crushed peppercorns and the flour and add a little salt. Slice the monkfish and press the peppercorn mixture onto it. When you are ready to eat, warm a large non-stick frying pan on a high heat. Add a little oil and a knob of butter and fry the fish carefully until the pieces are brown on both sides. Add the brandy and the port, and carefully set the contents of the pan alight. When the alcohol fumes have burnt off, reduce the heat and cover with foil. Continue to cook for a further three to five minutes depending on the thickness of the pieces. Remove the fish to a heated serving dish and boil the juices to reduce until they are syrupy. Finish the sauce by adding the double cream and stirring to amalgamate. Season the sauce to taste with a little salt, then pour over the fish.

ingredients

650g monkfish fillets sliced into long thick strips

1tbsp black peppercorns crushed

Large pinch of salt

2 tsp flour

A little butter and oil for cooking the fish

125ml brandy

175ml port

125ml double cream

Ginger and currant butter

This lovely butter can be made and frozen for use either with the salmon in pastry recipe on page 68 or using with grilled chicken or guinea fowl – it is very versatile.

method

Place the butter in a large bowl and beat lightly to soften it. Add the rest of the ingredients. Mix well and refrigerate or freeze until needed.

ingredients

25g stem ginger preserved in syrup, washed and finely chopped

100g unsalted butter at room temperature

25g currants

10g fresh ginger, finely grated

½ tsp lemon juice

Salt and pepper

Fillets of sole
steamed with ginger, lime and lemongrass

The flavour of sole is delicate, but its flesh is firm and delicious. This recipe gives a light dish suitable as a starter when a richer main course is to follow.

Serves 4 as a starter or two as a main course

method

Place a steamer over a pan of simmering water.

Mix together the lemongrass, ginger, lime and mushrooms and season well with salt and pepper. Spread the filling evenly over the fillets, roll up each portion of sole from the thin end and place on a buttered dish that will fit into the steamer. Steam the fish until the flesh is opaque and flakes easily (about eight minutes) and serve with herb hollandaise (see page 62).

ingredients

4 × 140g fillets of Dover or lemon sole

1 stem of lemongrass, very finely shredded

1 tsp fresh ginger, peeled and very finely grated

Zest and juice of ½ lime

115g oyster mushrooms, sliced thinly

Salt and pepper

A little butter for greasing the dish

Sweet and sour five willow sauce

This sauce is lovely served with freshly grilled mackerel or herring and makes enough for four people.

method

Heat the oil in a wide, shallow pan over a medium heat and sauté the vegetables lightly to soften them for a couple of minutes. Add the sugar, salt, fish stock, tomato paste and soy sauce and bring to the boil. Mix together the cornflour and vinegar to form a smooth paste and add it to the mixture, stirring well. Boil for one minute and season to taste.

ingredients

6 spring onions, shredded

2 red chillies, deseeded and finely shredded

40g pickled ginger, shredded

55g pickled gherkin, shredded

6 pickled onions, shredded

3 tbsp granulated sugar or palm sugar

½ tsp salt

300ml fish stock (see page 32)

4 tsp tomato paste

2 tsp soy sauce

3 tbsp peanut oil

1 tsp cornflour

4 tbsp vinegar

Seared salmon
with soured cream and dill served with a lime couscous salad

Only the best quality salmon such as Loch Duart or other RSPCA Freedom Food certified fish should be used for this dish. Such fish have a lower oil content which allows the fine flavour of the salmon to come to the fore.

Serves 4

method

Put the couscous into a bowl and pour on enough boiling water or vegetable stock to just cover it and set aside to cool. When it has, fork the couscous through, add the lime juice and mix. Set it aside while you cook the fish.

Mix together the soured cream with the dill, then season to taste with the lemon and a little salt and pepper.

Heat a skillet or heavy frying pan over a high heat to get really hot. Season the salmon fillets with a little salt, pepper and five spice, and drizzle with the oil. Put them on the skillet skin side down and cook for a couple of minutes until nicely brown. Turn the steaks over and continue to cook for another two or three minutes until the fish is cooked, when you will see that the flesh can be easily flaked apart. Serve on a bed of the couscous with a spoonful of the soured cream and a lemon garnish.

ingredients

225g couscous

Vegetable stock or water (see page 33)

Juice of one lime

4 × 115g salmon fillets, skin on, boned

2 tbsp groundnut oil

Pinch Chinese five-spice powder

Salt and freshly ground black pepper

To serve:

125ml soured cream

Lemon juice to taste

1 tbsp fresh dill, chopped

Salt and pepper

Lemon wedges

Gravadlax/bass

For gravadlax, it is important to get the best quality salmon you can afford – cheaper farmed salmon can be overly oily. Loch Duart and other RSPCA-approved salmon is available widely now and can be sourced from the addresses at the back of the book. This recipe involves curing the fish for three days, but requires only little preparation, so is easily made. At the restaurant we also made this dish with sea bass, which is delicious.

Serves 8

method

Place one of the pieces of salmon skin side down in a glass or ceramic dish. Combine the remaining ingredients and sprinkle them over the salmon. Place the other piece of salmon on top, skin side up. Cover with cling film and place a large plate or baking tray on top of the salmon and weigh it down with a couple of large tins or weights. Put it in the fridge. After 12 hours turn the fish over and baste the inside layers with any liquid that has formed in the dish. Do this every 12 hours for 72 hours in total.

To serve, scrape off the dill mixture, pat the fish dry and slice it very thinly, at an angle working from the tail end backwards. Dress with a dill and mustard sauce (see below) and some rye bread and lemon wedges on the side.

The gravadlax will keep for up to one week if well wrapped and kept chilled. Alternatively, the finished fish can be frozen for up to one month.

ingredients

2 × 650g pieces of salmon or equivalent of sea bass, skin on and pin boned

4 tbsp flaky sea salt

1½ tbsp caster sugar

1 tbsp juniper berries, crushed

1 tbsp black peppercorns crushed

Large bunch of dill, washed, dried and finely chopped

Dill and mustard sauce for gravadlax

Serves 4 as a starter.

method

Combine all the ingredients together in a small bowl and whisk until amalgamated. Drizzle over the gravadlax.

ingredients

6 tbsps light olive oil

1 tbsp cider vinegar

2 tsps Dijon mustard

1 tbsp dill, washed, dried and finely chopped

Salt and black pepper to taste

Skate
with shallot and apple cider

Skate is no longer commonly available as the stocks are much reduced in the past decade. Ray of various forms is still available, as is sustainable line-caught skate, so make sure you know what you are buying. This light brothy dish requires little accompaniment save for a green salad and crusty bread.

Serves 4

method

Preheat the oven to 150C/Gas mark 2.

Sweat the shallots in half the butter. Add the cider and fish stock and simmer gently until reduced by half. Season with a little salt and pepper and add the Calvados, apple and tomato. Put the skate into a buttered ovenproof dish and cover with the apple and cider mixture. Cover with tin foil and bake in the oven for about 12 minutes until the fish is tender (the actual time will depend on how thick the pieces are). If it is cooked, the flesh will easily pull away from the bones. Carefully remove the fish from the dish and put on a heated serving dish in a warm place while you finish the sauce. Transfer the juices to a pan over a high heat and simmer to reduce to a syrupy sauce. Finish the sauce by whisking in the rest of the butter and the mustard, then seasoning to taste. Pour over the fish.

ingredients

55g butter

2 large shallots, peeled and finely chopped

125ml medium dry cider

225ml fish stock (see page 32)

50ml Calvados

1 large cooking apple, peeled and diced

225g ripe tomatoes, peeled and diced

4 portions of ray or line-caught skate, about 150g each

1 tsp wholegrain mustard

Salt and pepper

Salmon in pastry
with ginger and currants

A classic dish, which appeared on the menu at the restaurant over many years. We only used the best salmon for it – that which swam along the river in front of the restaurant along the Dart. Now, good sources of sustainably farmed salmon are available and are well worth trying. Served with sauce Messine, this dish is a magnificent way to treat yourself and your guests.

Serves 4

method

Divide the fish into two horizontal slices and season with salt and pepper. Spread the ginger butter (see page 63) over both slices of fish and sandwich them together. Roll out the pastry into a thin sheet large enough to wrap around the salmon to make a neat parcel. Brush the pastry parcel with the beaten egg and chill if not baking immediately. When ready to cook, put it in an oven preheated to 220C/Gas mark 7 to bake for 30-40 minutes. Turn the heat down to 150C/Gas mark 2 half way through the cooking. The parcel is ready when it is evenly browned all over. Remove from the oven and allow it to rest for five minutes on top of the stove, then transfer to a warmed serving dish using a couple of fish slices, and serve with the sauce Messine (see below).

ingredients

900g fresh salmon fillet, skinned and boned

1 quantity ginger and currant butter (see page 63)

225g shortcrust pastry (see page 113)

1 egg, beaten, for the glaze

Salt and pepper

Sauce Messine

A delicious herb and mustard cream sauce that complements fish wonderfully. It is a natural partner to Salmon in Pastry (see above).

Makes 650ml serves 4-6

method

Heat the butter in a medium saucepan over a low to medium heat. When it melts, add the shallots and a pinch of salt and cook, stirring occasionally, so that the shallots soften but do not colour. Add the flour and cook, stirring, to amalgamate the ingredients. Reduce the heat to low and cook, stirring, for two minutes to cook the flour. Add the cream, in stages, and raise the heat to medium-high. The sauce will thicken a little with each addition, and you should let the sauce simmer between additions so that it cooks and remains free of lumps. When all the cream has been added, allow the sauce to simmer over a low heat for two or three minutes, then add the herbs and season to taste with salt and pepper. Add the mustard and lemon juice to taste, then serve with the fish.

ingredients

50g unsalted butter

2 shallots, peeled and finely chopped

½ tbsp each chopped chervil, tarragon and parsley

2 tsp plain flour

600ml single cream

Juice of ½ lemon

2 tsp Dijon or wholegrain mustard

Salt and black pepper

Ceviche

Delicate, lime scented fillets of sole or bass with a little chilli make a fresh starter for a summer meal. This can be served simply, as it comes out of the fridge, and laid out on chilled serving plates. For a more formal presentation, decorate with a little sliced avocado, some fresh fennel or chervil leaves and a dice of tiny tomatoes – but keep it to two or three additions or the simplicity of the dish will be lost.

This came to us from Jane Grigson, a real friend and one of our finest food writers.

Serves 6 as a starter

method

Cut the fish across the width of the fillets, on a bias, into thin slices or strips. Lay these in a box that has an airtight lid. Zest the limes using a fine grater and cover this in a small pot in the fridge.

Squeeze the limes – it can help to put them in a microwave for 30 seconds first – then cool the juice and pour it over the fish. Sprinkle the fish with a little salt and add the bay leaves, finely chopped chilli and onion, tucking them into the slices of fish. Cover the fish and chill it for four or five hours, during which time the acidic juice will denature the protein in the flesh, turning it opaque and giving it the appearance of being cooked.

To serve, drain the fish from its marinade and dress with a little light olive oil. Arrange on chilled serving plates and decorate with the reserved lime zest and slices of cucumber.

ingredients

500g Dover or lemon sole, or wild sea bass, skinned and filleted

Juice of 6 limes

Salt

2 bay leaves

1 hot red chilli, deseeded and finely chopped

1 medium red onion, peeled and finely sliced

A little light olive oil

Thinly sliced cucumber

69

Smoked fish tart

Crisp pastry and a creamy, aromatic filling make a perfect combination in this lovely tart. Use undyed smoked haddock which is widely available, or Finnan haddock if you are lucky enough to be able to buy it – it is the finest.

Serves 6

method

Preheat the oven to 200C/Gas mark 6.

Lightly grease a 20cm tart case and line it with thinly rolled shortcrust pastry, pressing it well into the corners. Allow the pastry to overlap the edges a little, but reserve any trimmings. Chill for ten to fifteen minutes, then line with non-stick baking parchment and fill with baking beans. Bake in a preheated oven for twenty minutes until the pastry is set, then remove the beans and return the tart to the oven and continue to cook the pastry until it is evenly browned. At this point, check that there are no holes in the case – if there are, simply fill them with a little of the pastry trimmings, smearing it into the cracks and return the case to the oven for five minutes.

While the pastry cooks, finely chop the smoked fish and season with a little lemon juice, salt and pepper. Put the fish into the pastry case. Mix together the milk, cream, eggs and egg yolks and season well. Pour the liquid into the pastry case and bake in a hot oven (preheated to 220C/Gas mark 7) for 20 minutes and then reduce the heat to 170C/Gas mark 3 for another 20 minutes or until set and lightly browned.

ingredients

Butter for greasing

Shortcrust pastry (see page 113) made with 225g plain flour and 115g butter

115g smoked salmon or haddock

150ml single cream

150ml milk

2 eggs

2 egg yolks

Lemon juice

Salt and pepper

Salt cod fishcakes

Salt cod can be made into delicious fishcakes which are richly aromatic. Serve these with a salad of ripe tomatoes dressed with a little extra virgin olive oil and a sharp, light white wine.

Serves 4

method

Cut the salt cod into four pieces. Cut up the potato into as evenly-sized pieces as possible, about the size of a walnut. Put the potatoes and cod into a pan and cover with cold water. Bring to the boil and simmer gently until the potatoes are cooked. Remove the fish from the pan, drain the potatoes and mash. Flake the cod and add to the potatoes along with the herbs, lemon juice, egg and pepper. Mix well and check for seasoning. Now shape the mixture into four even cakes about 6cm across and 2.5cm thick. To cook, heat a non-stick pan on a medium to high heat, add a little olive oil and fry the cakes two at a time on both sides until they are well browned. Transfer them as they are cooked to a heated serving dish and keep warm while you finish cooking them all. Serve with a plain or herb hollandaise and lemon wedges.

ingredients

225g salt cod, soaked overnight in several changes of water, then drained

225g peeled potatoes

2 tbsp chopped parsley or dill

Juice of ½ lemon

1 egg, beaten

Pepper

A little light olive oil for cooking

To serve:

Lemon wedges

Herb hollandaise or aioli (see pages 62 and 61)

Prawn sesame toasts

These little toasts make lovely accompaniments to drinks and can be prepared mostly in advanced. They simply require frying at the last minute.

method

Put three slices of bread into the bowl of a food processor and reduce to breadcrumbs. Add the prawns, ginger, egg, cornflour, sherry and seasoning and purée finely. Then transfer the mixture to a bowl, add 1 tbsp sesame seeds and stir to combine.

Remove the crusts from the rest of the bread. Spread the paste on the bread and then cut each piece into four fingers or 12 squares.

To cook, heat a deep fat fryer to 160C, or heat 1 cm oil in a deep, large frying pan and use a temperature probe to monitor the temperature. Do not leave the oil unattended even for a minute. Then transfer the toasts to the oil a few at a time and cook until they are golden brown on both sides. Remove from the oil and drain on kitchen paper until all the toasts are cooked. Serve hot.

ingredients

225g peeled prawns

1 inch piece root ginger

1 egg

2 tbsp cornflour

1 tbsp sherry

7 slices white bread, crusts removed

1 tbsp sesame seeds

Salt and pepper

Sunflower oil for cooking

Freshly cooked lobsters

Freshly cooked lobster is a super treat, one that should be savoured. Don't be afraid of cooking a lobster at home – they are straightforward but need timing carefully so that the flesh does not overcook. As a rule of thumb, cook lobster for 15 minutes per kilo in gently simmering water.

When organising lobsters for yourself and your guests, reckon on half a 750g lobster per person for a starter, or one 600-800g lobster per person for a main course.

Killing the shellfish

Care should be taken to kill the lobster before it is cooked. You can ask your fishmonger to do this for you, but you can also learn to do it yourself. First, bring a large pan of water to the boil and add salt in the ratio 1 tbsp for every 4 litres water. To kill the lobster, you need to cut through its nerve cord, which is immediately underneath a cross that you will see about half way down the animal's head. Using a sharp knife, pierce this cross, pushing the tip of the knife all the way through. The lobster will twitch, but will be killed.

If you are planning to cook more than one lobster, cook just two at a time – any more and the water will take too long to come back to a boil.

Place the lobster in the simmering water and put the lid onto the pan. Allow the pan to come back to a gentle simmer and time your lobster to cook for 15 minutes per kilo. When the lobster is cooked, remove it from the water and put it in a bowl under a running cold tap. Allow the lobster to cool for five minutes, then refrigerate until completely cold.

To prepare the lobster

Lay the cooked lobster on a board. Remove the claws where they are joined to the body. Have the lobster with its head to the left. With a strong stainless steel knife split the lobster down the body starting at the head and finishing at the tail. Lay the halves out, then remove the stomach sac from the head (this may have pieces of shell in it) and the intestine tube which runs down the back of the animal just under the top surface of the shell.

Inside the head you will see some brown, creamy flesh, called tomalley. This is the delicious brown meat of the lobster. It can be left in place or spooned out into a bowl and used for making Courchamps Sauce (see below). If you see a line of red flesh running from the lobster head into the tail meat, do not be alarmed. This will appear in female specimens and is the coral, or forming eggs. This can be spooned out and mixed into a little butter, which can then be used to enrich a sauce or risotto.

Crack the claws and remove the flesh, keeping it as whole as possible and arrange it on the head, then transfer the lobster halves to a serving dish.

To serve one very large lobster, prepare as before and, when boiled and cooled, remove all the flesh from the tail and the claws. Portion according to the number of guests, allowing each person a fair share of the tail and claw meat. You will also find a great deal of meat in the feelers where they and the claws join the head. Remove the tomalley from the head with a spoon and reserve for the sauce. The smaller pickings of the lobster can be saved for a mousse or potted lobster or a superior fish cake or cutlet.

We like to present lobster as cleanly as possible, with a sauce on the side rather than mixed into the meat. Serve with a good mayonnaise (see next page) or with Courchamps sauce made with the tomalley. We also enjoy it with Alan Davidson's South East Asian combination of mango and horseradish (see next page).

Mango and horseradish sauce

Serves 4

method

In a bowl, mix together the mango, horseradish and mayonnaise and thin out with a little single cream. Season to taste with salt, pepper, sugar and a little lemon juice.

ingredients

225g prepared cubed mango

175g mayonnaise

1 tbsp grated horseradish

60ml single cream

Salt and pepper

Squeeze of lemon juice

Pinch of sugar

Herb mayonnaise

This basic recipe can be adapted to suit whichever herbs you have available. Basil, chervil, tarragon, parsley, fennel and chives can all be used in combination.

Serves 4

method

Put the egg and a little seasoning into a blender. Have the oils ready in a jug and set the blender going. Gradually add the oils in a thin stream until all the oil has been added and emulsified. Add the herbs and run the blender until they are finely chopped. Put the mayonnaise into a bowl and add the lemon juice, mix well and check the seasoning. Serve with fresh crab, lobster or prawns.

ingredients

3 tbsp soft herbs, chopped

Juice of ½ lemon

150ml light olive oil

150ml groundnut oil

1 egg at room temperature

Salt and cayenne pepper

Courchamps sauce

Serves 4

method

Put all the ingredients except the lemon juice into a food processor or blender and blend well. Add the lemon juice and then check for seasoning. This sauce can also be added to an equal amount of mayonnaise to accompany shellfish such as freshly cooked prawns.

ingredients

2 tbsp tomalley (the brown meat from the head of a lobster)

2 tbsp Pernod, or similar anise liqueur

1 tsp soy sauce

1 tsp chopped parsley

1 tsp chopped tarragon

1 tsp Dijon mustard

4 tbsp olive oil

Juice of ½ lemon

Salt and pepper

Stuffed mussels

At the restaurant we used to cook these lovely stuffed mussels in one of two ways, either with spinach and cream, or with lemon and shallot butter. They make a super canapé or nibble either way – just serve them with cocktail sticks for people to pick out the flesh. For the lemon and shallot butter, see page 76.

Remember to discard any mussels that will not close when tapped before cooking, and any that remain closed when cooked.

Serves 4 as an appetizer

method

Heat a large pan over a high heat, then add the butter and the spinach. Cook, stirring until the spinach collapses and softens. Remove from the heat and transfer to a colander. Squeeze out any excess water and discard. Return the spinach to the pan, add the double cream and cook again. Season with salt, pepper and nutmeg. Transfer the spinach into a food processor and purée.

To cook the mussels, heat a large pan on a high heat. Put the clean, de-bearded mussels in a large bowl with 100ml water and add the whole bowlful to the hot pan, being careful to avoid any steam that gushes up. Cook for three or four minutes until they are all opened up. Transfer them to a colander set over a large bowl and drain. Discard the liquid.

Remove one wing of each shell, spread a little of the spinach paste over the mussel with a palette knife and then lay them on an oven proof tray. Top with a few of the breadcrumbs and a small piece of butter on each one.

Bake in an oven preheated to 200C/Gas mark 6 for five minutes and then brown under the grill before serving.

ingredients

1.2 litres mussels, washed and de-bearded

225g spinach, washed well

15g unsalted butter

Dash of double cream

Salt, pepper and nutmeg

100g soft breadcrumbs

30g unsalted butter, diced for topping

Hot and sour shellfish broth

This soup is inspired by Nick Coiley, our head chef for many years, who travelled widely in Asia.

Avoid any mussels that will not close when tapped before cooking, and any that remain closed when cooked.

Serves 4-6

method

Heat the vegetable oil in a large pan over a medium heat, add the onions and the garlic, and fry, stirring, until they are lightly browned. Add the mussels and then turn the heat up, cover and cook for three to five minutes or until the mussels have all opened. Lift the mussels out with a slotted spoon and set aside to cool. Add the chicken stock, lime leaves, lemongrass and ginger to the pan. Pull the leaves from the stalks of the coriander, cut the stalks into pieces and add them to the broth, setting the leaves aside. Bring the broth to the boil and cover tightly, lower the heat and simmer gently for 30 minutes.

Add the vinegar and sugar and simmer for a few more minutes. Strain the broth into a pan, pressing to get out all the juices. Return the pan to the heat and add the scallops, prawns, mussels, lime juice, mixed arrowroot and water, and fish sauce. Bring to a simmer over a high heat and then add the chillies, coriander leaves, salt and pepper. Remove from the heat and leave to infuse for five minutes. Serve into warmed bowls, distributing the shellfish evenly between your diners.

ingredients

2 tbsp sunflower oil

225g onions, peeled and chopped

4 cloves garlic, peeled and sliced

900g mussels, scrubbed and de-bearded

600ml chicken stock (see page 31)

2 stalks lemongrass, finely chopped

6 lime leaves, torn in pieces

5cm piece root ginger, peeled and sliced

1 bunch (approx 60g) fresh coriander washed and dried

3 tbsp rice vinegar or white wine vinegar

1 tsp granulated sugar

Juice of 2 limes

4 tbsp Thai fish sauce

4 scallops, halved

450g raw prawns, peeled

1 tsp arrowroot mixed with a little water

3 hot green chillies, deseeded and chopped

Crab cakes

Brown crabs in our cold deep waters produce some of the best flavoured seafood in the world. The rich, sweet flesh is unparalleled and so flavourful that it combines well with any number of ingredients. These little crab cakes are best served as a light lunch or supper dish with a salad of peeled cucumber dressed with soured cream and chopped chives.

Serves 4 as a starter

method

Put all the ingredients except for one third of the breadcrumbs into a large bowl and mix well. Shape the mixture into eight even cakes using your fingers and a large spoon, then coat in the breadcrumbs. Chill unless you intend to cook the cakes immediately. To cook, heat a little olive oil in a large non-stick frying pan and cook the cakes until they are brown on both sides and piping hot.

Serve with a cucumber, soured cream and chive salad.

ingredients

225g picked crab meat, brown and white mixed

1 egg, beaten lightly

1 tbsp soured cream

2 tsp wholegrain mustard

Sprig of fresh coriander, chopped

1 spring onion, finely chopped

85g soft white breadcrumbs

Zest of 1 lime

Juice of ½ lemon

Salt and pepper

Lemon shallot butter

This butter can be used to top mussels in the same way as the spinach and cream mixture recipe on page 74, finished with breadcrumbs and then grilled or baked.

method

Heat a medium pan over a medium heat and add a small knob of the butter. Add the chopped shallots and cook, stirring, until they soften but do not colour. Add the white wine and turn the heat up to medium high. Allow the mixture to cook until it has all reduced, then remove from the heat. Transfer the shallots to the bowl of a food processor along with the butter, lemon juice, zest and parsley, and blend to make a spreadable butter.

ingredients

2 shallots, peeled and finely chopped

115g unsalted butter

Zest and juice of ½ lemon

125ml light white wine

25g parsley, finely chopped

Crab spring rolls
with sweet chilli sauce

These little rolls make super snack food to serve with drinks in place of a sit-down starter. The rolls can be prepared in advance, then fried at the last minute.

Serves 6 with drinks

method

Put the water, sugar, chilli and juice in a pan and bring to the boil. Add the vinegar mixture and then bring back to the boil and keep boiling until the mixture starts to thicken. Remove from the heat and serve hot or cold.

When the sauce is ready, cook the noodles for the filling according to the instructions on the packet.

In a bowl, mix all the ingredients for the filling with the chopped noodles and season well. Put a spoonful of filling at one end of a wrapper laid on the diagonal. Fold in the corners on both sides so that you have a rectangle and then roll up, moistening the end with a little water to seal. Repeat until the mixture is all finished. As you work, place the finished rolls onto a baking tray lined with cling film.

When all of the rolls are finished, put your deep fat fryer on to heat, or heat 1.5 litres oil in a large pan set over a high heat, and heat to 160C. If you are using a pan, do not leave the pan alone at any point. Deep fry the rolls a few at a time until they are a rich golden brown, then drain well on kitchen paper. Keep them warm while you cook the whole batch, then serve with the chilli dipping sauce.

ingredients

1 packet spring roll wrappers

For the filling:

115g glass noodles, blanched, or egg noodles, cooked

225g crab meat, brown and white, roughly chopped

1 tsp chilli oil or sesame oil

Splash of Thai fish sauce

Zest and juice of ½ lime

1 tsp soy sauce

55g baby corn, finely chopped

115g bean sprouts, chopped

1 bunch (approx 60g) fresh coriander, washed and dried

1 tbsp chopped chives

1 tbsp chopped basil

1 small piece of root ginger, peeled and finely grated

For the sauce:

300ml water

115g sugar

1 chopped red chilli

Juice of 1 lemon or 2 limes

½ tsp cornflour dissolved in 2 tsp cider or white wine vinegar

1.5 litres sunflower or groundnut oil for frying

Potted crab

This traditional recipe has ginger added to spice up the crab – one of Joyce's favourite flavourings. The resulting potted mixture is best eaten within two or three days, but requires chilling, so make it at least four or five hours before you intend to eat it to allow the butter to set.

Serves 4 as a starter

method

In a large bowl, mix the crab with the lemon juice, herbs and seasoning and add the melted butter. Stir to combine thoroughly. Line six 100ml ramekins with cling film, and divide the mixture between them. Cover the ramekins with cling film and chill.

When ready to serve, remove the cling film cover, turn out each ramekin onto a plate and remove the cling film lining. Serve with hot brown toast and watercress.

ingredients

225g crab meat, brown and white mixed

175g unsalted butter, melted

Pinch ground mace

Juice of ½ lemon

1 tsp grated fresh ginger

1 tbsp chopped parsley

Salt and pepper

To serve:
Wholemeal toast and fresh watercress

Mussels with white wine

This super recipe is simple and delicious. Mussels are widely available during the winter months, when they are at their best. When buying, look for small, even sized shells – these are the sweetest. Discard any that will not close when tapped before cooking, and do not eat any that remain closed when cooked.

Serves 8 as a starter or 4 as a main course

method

Place the butter in a large pan over a medium heat. When it melts, add the shallots and cook, stirring for two or three minutes until they are sizzling and beginning to soften. Add the rest of the ingredients except the mussels, bring the pan to a simmer and then reduce by half.

Put a clean large pan on a high heat to get hot. Put the cleaned mussels into a large bowl with the reduced sauce. Tip into the hot, empty pan, being careful to avoid any steam as it gushes up, and put the lid on. Cook the mussels, shaking occasionally, for three to four minutes until they open. Add the double cream and seasoning.

ingredients

1.8kg mussels, washed and de-bearded

8 shallots, peeled and finely chopped

55g unsalted butter

300ml light white wine

300ml fish stock

2 bay leaves

2 tbsp chopped parsley

Sprig of thyme

100ml double cream

Salt and pepper

Stir fried squid
with noodles

Ask your fishmonger to prepare the squid for you by removing the internal mantle and intestines. This is a super, quick way of cooking squid.

Serves 4 as a starter

method

Have all the ingredients ready before you begin to cook. Mix the Thai fish sauce, soy, stock or water and lemon juice in a small bowl, and prepare all the vegetables.

Just before you are ready to cook the squid, which only take four or five minutes from start to finish, cook the noodles according to the instructions on the packet, then drain and keep them warm on a heated serving dish.

Heat a wok or a large deep frying pan over a high heat and add the oils. When the wok is smoking, add the ginger, garlic, peppers and squid and stir-fry quickly to combine thoroughly. Add the liquid and stir, cook for one or two minutes and then add the coriander, lemon juice, and seasoning. Toss the mixture together carefully and then serve on top of the hot noodles.

ingredients

225g sliced raw squid tubes and tentacles

1 clove garlic, finely chopped

1 tbsp root ginger, finely chopped

1 tbsp groundnut oil

1 tsp chilli oil

1 tsp sesame oil

225g cooked egg noodles

175g sliced red pepper

2 tbsp Thai fish sauce

1 tbsp soy sauce

4 tbsp fish stock or water (see page 32)

Juice of ½ lemon

1 tbsp chopped coriander

Salt and pepper

Marinated scallops
with lime and basil

Only use the freshest scallops for this recipe. The sweet, natural flesh marries beautifully with the lime dressing.

method

Whisk together the lime juice and zest, the oils, the herbs and a little salt and pepper. Put the scallops into a dish and pour over the marinade. Cover the dish with cling film and refrigerate. Leave the scallops to marinate for at least two or three hours.

Serve, not too cold, with some blanched samphire or some watercress or shaved asparagus.

ingredients

12 scallops, each sliced into three horizontal discs

Zest and juice of 4 lime

125ml olive oil

30ml sesame oil

1 tbsp chopped chives

1 tbsp chopped coriander

2 tbsp chopped basil

Salt and pepper

Scallops with sorrel sauce

Large-leaved French sorrel is an easy herb to keep in the garden or a pot. Its large succulent leaves have the texture of spinach, albeit with a lighter colour. Their lemony acidity makes an excellent foil for rich shellfish. Once the sorrel has flowered, in midsummer, cut the leaves back and give the plant a good feed. You will be rewarded with a vigorous second crop of leaves.

Serves 4 as a starter or 2 as a main course

method

Put the shallots in a medium saucepan with the fish stock and white wine and place on a high heat. Bring to a boil and cook until the mixture is reduced by two thirds.

Transfer the reduction to a blender and add the egg, the sorrel and a little seasoning. Start the blender going and slowly pour in the hot butter. When all the butter has been added you should have a lightly thickened sauce. Check the seasoning. Gently pour the sauce into a bowl over a pan of hot, but not boiling water and keep it warm while you cook the scallops.

Trim the scallops and lay them on a board in front of you. Season lightly with salt and black pepper and drizzle over a little light olive oil. Heat a large non-stick pan or skillet over a high heat, and when it is really hot, add the scallops. Leave them in place for 30 seconds or so to pick up colour, then flip each in turn and cook for another 30-40 seconds. Divide them between your plates and serve with the warm sorrel sauce.

ingredients

8-12 prepared scallops

1 egg, beaten lightly

55g prepared sorrel

55g shallots, peeled and finely chopped

55ml fish stock (see page 32)

55ml white wine

85g unsalted butter, melted and heated to boiling

Salt and pepper

Poultry

Chicken was once a luxury for us to cook at home, and it would be nice to see people taking more care to source well-produced, flavourful poultry instead of the mass produced, tasteless birds that are produced under poor conditions. Properly free range and organic birds, where they are free to roam out of doors, grow more slowly, taste far better and are worth looking out for.

It is almost always worth buying a whole bird and asking your butcher to portion it for you, giving you the carcass and trimmings for stock, which can be amassed in the freezer until you have a sufficient quantity to fill your stockpot. That way, you can get the most economical use of what you buy. Recipes for stocks can be found in the chapter on soups.

Chicken has a flavour that can take almost any accompaniment, it is mild and delicate and balances richer or spicy flavours well. We have given recipes that show this versatility, from a rich 'Coq au Vin' to 'spiced chicken wings' and 'sticky drumsticks' which make good picnic or barbecue food.

Ducks are less often sold fresh, but you should ask your butcher for specific varieties. The domestic Gressingham ducks are well worth searching out because they combine a good size with excellent flavour. Relatively inexpensive, duck legs can be made into flavoursome, elaborate dishes that make them seem very special, as they are when stuffed with apricots and braised with red wine in one of our recipes. Poultry offal, too, gives great flavour for money value, made here into a fine parfait that is delicate enough to grace any table.

Duck legs stuffed with apricots
and braised in red wine

Anyone can master this recipe with a little patience, and it is well worth trying.
Duck legs have a lovely flavour and a melting texture once cooked.

Serves 4

method

First make the stuffing. Heat the duck fat in a medium frying pan over a
medium heat. Add the onion and a pinch of salt and cook, stirring occasionally
until it softens and becomes clear, then add the thyme. Add the apricots,
orange juice and brandy and cook them all together over a low heat until the
apricots are plump and have absorbed all the liquid. If the mixture dries, but
the apricots are still hard, add a cupful of water and continue to cook until
the apricots are soft. Remove from the heat, cool, add the breadcrumbs and
season to taste.

While the stuffing is cooking, prepare the duck legs. Lay them on a chopping
board in front of you, skin side down. You will see that the skin extends
beyond the meat and has some thickened patches of fat. The fat is best
removed but you do not want to remove the skin, so, using a sharp knife, trim
any excess fat working the blade horizontally between the fat and the skin,
reserving any trimmings for frying later. Then look at the bones. You will see the
knee joint half way down the leg. A bone extends from this to the widest part
of the thigh, where the leg was attached to the pelvis. You need to remove this
bone in order to create a small pocket to take the stuffing. To do this, run the
tip of a sharp knife along each side of the bone, then cut carefully under the

bone to free it from the meat of the thigh. Then, snap the knee joint and cut any tendons that stop you removing the bone. You should be left with just one bone intact in the drumstick. Keep the bones you have removed, as they are used later.

Next, stuff the legs. Divide the apricot stuffing between the four legs, piling it into the small cavity you have created by removing the bone. Pull the skin and thigh meat over the filling, covering it completely and, using a large needle and some cotton thread, sew up the legs, tying each firmly so that the stuffing is completely enclosed. If you need to remove any, so be it. Wipe the legs clean of any stuffing that clings to the skin.

The legs now need to be browned before they are braised. Heat the remaining duck fat in a large frying pan or casserole over a medium to high heat. Place the legs in the pan, skin side down, cook until they are a deep brown on the skin side, then turn them over. When they are all evenly brown on both sides – it will take eight minutes or so in total – remove the legs and all but a tablespoon of the fat. Add the chopped vegetables and fry over a medium to high heat until they are well browned. Add the flour and tomato purée and stir so that the flour is combined with no lumps. Add the stock, wine, seasoning and herbs and bring to a simmer. Place the legs and all their accompanying juices and vegetables in a casserole and bake in a low oven (150C/Gas mark 3) for about one hour until cooked through. Remove the legs from the liquid and set aside on a warm plate, then strain the sauce through a fine sieve into a clean pan. Remove the cotton from the legs and slice them in half. Serve with a simple root vegetable purée, and the sauce, reduced if necessary, with the seasoning checked.

ingredients

4 boned duck legs (see method)

1 onion, finely chopped

1 tbsp duck fat or unsalted butter

1 carrot, peeled and finely diced

1 stick celery, finely diced

1 sprig each fresh thyme and parsley and 1 bay leaf, tied together

300ml light red wine

300ml duck or chicken stock (see page 31)

1 level tsp plain flour

1 tsp tomato purée

For the stuffing:

115g dried sliced apricots

Juice of ½ orange

1 large onion, finely chopped

15g butter or duck fat

2 tsp chopped fresh thyme

15g soft fresh breadcrumbs

1 tbsp brandy

Salt and pepper

Duck liver parfait

This super-fine paté is a delight that can be made a couple of days in advance – a real boost for the kitchen. It is aromatic and delicious.

Serves 8-10

method

Place a large frying pan on a medium heat and add 1 tsp butter. When it melts, add the onion and garlic and a pinch of salt. Cook, stirring, until the vegetables become tender. Add the thyme, brandy, Madeira and port and boil until there is no liquid left, but not so much that the vegetables begin to burn. Remove from the heat and place the mixture in the jug of a liquidizer. To this, add the livers, eggs and melted butter and season with ½ tsp salt and plenty of black pepper. Blend until very smooth then pass through a fine sieve, pushing the mixture through with a ladle.

Preheat the oven to 150C/Gas mark 3.

Sprinkle a large loaf tin with water and line it with a large sheet of cling film, allowing it to overlap the edges on all sides. Pour the mixture into the tin, and cover the mixture with the excess cling film. Put in a bain-marie and cook in the oven for 45 minutes, or until a skewer pushed into the mixture comes out hot to the touch, or until a temperature probe inserted into the core registers 65C. When it is cooked, remove the tin from the oven and the loaf tin from the water. Transfer to a large tin of cold water – with ice if you have it – to cool the parfait as quickly as possible. Chill it, and when ready to serve, turn it out from the tin, remove the cling film and slice with a sharp knife dipped in boiling water. Transfer to plates and eat with cornichons or pickles and toast.

ingredients

200g duck or chicken livers, preferably organic

4 shallots or 1 large onion, chopped

1 clove garlic, finely chopped

1 sprig of fresh thyme

30ml brandy

45ml Madeira

45ml port

2 whole eggs

1 egg yolk

200g unsalted butter, melted

Salt and pepper

Chicken with three spices

Lightly spiced, this recipe is simple, creamy and aromatic. Serve with steamed basmati rice and a tomato salad for a simple supper. This dish could work equally well with skinned chicken breasts.

method

Place the cardamom seeds, cumin and coriander in a mortar or spice grinder and grind to a fine powder.

Place the butter in a medium frying pan over a medium heat. Add the onion and a pinch of salt. Cook, stirring until the onion is lightly browned, then season the chicken with a little salt and black pepper and add it to the pan. Add the spices and cook, stirring, until the chicken has all turned white but is not coloured.

Add the stock to the pan, cover and cook on a low heat for 15-20 minutes or until the pieces of chicken are cooked. To check this, pierce a thick piece with a sharp knife. If the juices run clear then it is cooked, but if the juices are pink or red, continue to cook until they run clear. Lift the lid from the pan and remove the chicken pieces and set aside. Bring the pan to a boil over a high heat and reduce the volume by half. Add the cream and reduce by half again. Turn the heat to low and return the chicken to the pan. Taste and adjust seasoning, and add the lemon juice. Stir, taste again, and serve.

ingredients

1.8kg free range chicken, skinned and jointed

1 tsp whole coriander seeds

1 tsp whole cumin seeds

1 tsp whole cardamom pods, seeds extracted and reserved

1 large onion, chopped

25g unsalted butter

Salt and pepper

Juice of half a lemon

150ml chicken stock 1 (see page 31)

150ml double cream

Peeled and sliced mango to serve

Coq au vin

A classic French braise that is a real treat – make sure you source the best chicken you can afford to get the best flavour and texture.

method

Heat half the butter in a large frying pan over a medium to high heat. Add the onions and bacon and cook, stirring for five to six minutes until they are well browned. Remove the onions and bacon to a bowl and add the remaining butter to the pan. Toss the chicken pieces in the flour on a plate and add to the pan. Let the pieces cook and brown, turning them so that they are all coloured well. Add the brandy, remove from the heat and set the fumes alight with a match, being careful to avoid any overhanging curtains or blinds! When the flames die down, return the pan to the heat and boil to reduce the juices. Remove the chicken pieces to a warm plate, add the remaining flour to the pan and stir to amalgamate until there is no flour visible.

Add the red wine and bring to a boil. Add the bay, thyme and garlic, and the onion and bacon mixture. Add the chicken and lightly season to taste. Cover the pan and simmer on a very low heat for 20 minutes. Add the button mushrooms and cook for a further five minutes. Taste, check for seasoning and remove from the heat. Insert a knife into the thickest part of the chicken and look at the juices. If they are clear, the dish is cooked. If they are pink, return the pan to a low heat and continue to simmer the mixture for ten minutes, then retest. The chicken should then be cooked. Transfer to a warmed serving dish and serve with boiled potatoes and a green salad or steamed, buttered carrots.

ingredients

1.8kg free range chicken, skinned and jointed

12 button mushrooms, wiped

12 small pickling onions or shallots, peeled

1 bottle Burgundy

2 tbsp brandy

115g dry-cured streaky bacon in strips

75g unsalted butter

25g plain flour

1 bay leaf

1 large sprig thyme

2 cloves garlic, peeled and finely chopped

Salt and pepper

Chicken with olives, anchovies and tomatoes

A summer dish par excellence, this can be served alongside a Provençal rosé from Bandol such as Domaine Tempier, one of the best producers of Mourvèdre.

method

Season the chicken joints with the salt and pepper. Heat the oil in a large non-stick frying pan over a medium high heat and add the chicken pieces. Fry these until they are well browned all over. Add the thyme and marjoram and the wine and bring to a boil, then add the tomatoes, olives, garlic and anchovies and simmer. Either cover and reduce the heat to low, or transfer the contents of the pan to a casserole and place the dish in an oven preheated to 150C/Gas mark 3. Cook the chicken for 20-25 minutes until the meat is cooked.

Insert a knife into the thickest part of the chicken and look at the juices. If they are clear, the dish is cooked. If they are pink, return the pan to a low heat and continue to simmer the mixture for 10 minutes, then retest. The chicken should then be cooked. Transfer to a warmed serving dish and sprinkle with the lemon juice and chopped parsley.

ingredients

1.8kg free range chicken, jointed

2 tbsp olive oil

1 tbsp chopped fresh thyme

1 tbsp chopped fresh marjoram or oregano

4 cloves garlic, peeled and finely chopped

175ml dry white wine

8 anchovy fillets, drained from their oil

400g tinned tomatoes, chopped

24 black olives, stones removed

1 large bunch parsley, washed and finely chopped

Juice of ½ lemon

Salt and pepper

Duck or pheasant leg confit

Duck legs have a huge amount of flavour and, when salted and slowly braised in this recipe, will keep for a several weeks in a very cold fridge. They can also be frozen, so it is worth making a large batch.

method

To prepare the duck legs, cut three or four slits in each and stuff the slits with garlic and thyme leaves. Place the legs in a dish and cover with a light sprinkling of sea salt. Leave covered overnight.

The next day, remove the duck from the dish and shake off any surplus salt. Place the legs in a roasting tin so that they just fit snugly and add the duck fat. Place the tin in a low oven, preheated to 150C/Gas mark 3, for two hours, turning the legs half way through.

Drain the legs from the fat and pour the fat through a sieve into a large jug, where the liquid will separate leaving the fat on top. Place the legs into a large jar or pot and pour over the melted fat to cover the legs, pressing them down well. Be careful not to include any of the liquid from underneath the fat. Cover the jars and store in the fridge for up to one month.

TO USE AND SERVE

When you are ready to serve the duck, remove the legs from the fat and reheat under the grill in a pan until the skin is crisp. Drain off any excess fat. Remove the legs and add 50ml chicken stock, 50ml orange juice and 1 tsp white wine vinegar per leg to the pan. Place over a high heat and boil to reduce the liquid by half. Add a knob or two of unsalted butter, stirring to melt. Take the meat off the bone and slice into large chunks, put on top of a little dressed salad and pour over the sauce. Finish with orange sections.

ingredients

8 duck or pheasant legs

40g sea salt

2 cloves garlic, peeled and chopped

3 bay leaves

Sprig of thyme, leaves removed and reserved

500g duck, goose or pork fat

To serve:

50ml chicken stock per leg (see page 31

50ml orange juice per leg

1 tsp white wine vinegar per leg

Unsalted butter

Salad and orange sections

Cornbreads

method

Preheat the oven to 200C/Gas mark 7.

Slice the baby corn finely, or cut the kernels from the ear of sweet corn and put in a bowl. Add the rest of the ingredients and mix well. Grease 12 non-stick muffin tins with a little duck fat or vegetable oil and fill with the mixture. Cook in a moderate oven until risen, golden, and springy to the touch.

ingredients

2 ears sweet corn, or 150g baby corn, trimmed

½ tsp chilli oil

1 tbsp root ginger, peeled and finely chopped

½ tsp baking powder

2 tbsp sugar

140g fine polenta

350ml duck or chicken stock (see page 31), or milk

3 eggs

Braised duck

Oriental spices combine well with the richness of duck, and this dish is a real favourite. We have incorporated many eastern flavours in our food over the years, enjoying the layers of spice and aromatic vegetables, and the way they give a great depth of flavour to our food.

method

Preheat the oven to 150C/Gas mark 3.

Place a large, non-stick frying pan on a medium to high heat. Add the duck fat and when it melts, add the duck pieces. Cook the duck until it is well browned on all sides, adding a pinch of salt. Remove the duck legs from the pan and transfer to a casserole. Drain the fat from the frying pan and reserve for future use. Add the remaining ingredients to the pan, bring to a simmer then pour over the duck pieces. Place a lid on the casserole and put in the oven. Cook for one hour.

Lift the legs from the liquid and remove the meat from the bones, carefully, so that the shape of the leg is retained. Strain the liquid and transfer to a clean bowl. Cool, cover and refrigerate both the legs and the liquid. When chilled, remove the fat from the surface of the stock and add to your store of duck fat. To serve, place the meat and stock in a medium saucepan and warm over a medium heat. Bring to a gentle simmer for five minutes to heat the mixture through thoroughly, then serve with cornbreads and pineapple pickle (see recipes below and page 92).

ingredients

2 tbsp duck fat

2 ducks, jointed, or 8 duck legs

750ml dark chicken stock (see page 31)

2 tbsp fresh lemongrass, finely chopped

1 tsp fresh ginger, peeled and finely chopped

2 tbsp sundried tomatoes, roughly chopped

1 tbsp dried thyme

2 tbsp sherry

3 tbsp soy sauce

3 tbsp apple or fruit jelly

2 sprigs fresh rosemary, roughly chopped

Salt and pepper

Pineapple pickle

method

Mix all ingredients together. Store in the fridge for up to one week.

ingredients

1 x 500g fresh pineapple, peeled, cored and finely diced

1 clove garlic, peeled and finely chopped

1 inch piece of ginger, peeled and finely chopped

1 tsp chilli oil

1 tbsp white mustard seeds

Pinch of turmeric

150ml white wine vinegar

Pinch of salt

Grilled spiced chicken
with yoghurt and turmeric sauce

An easy weekend dish, informal and delicious.

Serves 6

method

Grind the spices and mix with the ginger, salt and olive oil. Put under the skin of the chicken and either grill on a barbecue or place in a roasting tin and bake in an oven preheated to 200C/Gas mark 7 for 20 minutes.

To make the sauce, heat the oil in a large non-stick frying pan over a low to medium heat. Cook, stirring occasionally for five minutes or until the onion is soft and clear but not browned. Add the turmeric and ginger and fry again. Add the cream, currants, yoghurt, seasoning and lemon juice. Reheat gently over a low heat – you do not want the yoghurt to curdle – and serve with the grilled chicken.

Garnish with chopped fresh coriander.

ingredients

6 chicken breasts, off the bone and with the skin left on

1 tbsp coriander seeds, lightly roasted in a dry frying pan

1 tbsp cardamom, hulled, seeds retained

1 tbsp olive oil

1 tsp cloves

50g fresh ginger, peeled and finely grated

12 peppercorns

For the sauce:

A little groundnut or sunflower oil

1 onion, peeled and finely chopped

½ tsp turmeric

½ tsp fresh ginger peeled and grated

300ml full fat natural yoghurt

50ml double cream

1 tbsp currants (optional)

1 tsp lemon juice

Fresh coriander to garnish

Fried chicken wings
with cumin and coriander

These lightly spiced wings complement a cool drink on a hot day.

method

Grind the spices in a grinder or a pestle and mortar and coat the wings. Sprinkle with a good pinch of salt. To cook, heat 1cm oil in a large non-stick frying pan over a medium heat, then fry the wings until well browned all over. Drain on kitchen paper, then serve with soured cream or yoghurt as a dip or dressing for a snack.

ingredients

8 chicken wings

4 tsp cumin

4 tsp coriander

Pinch of salt

Groundnut oil for frying

Soured cream or yoghurt for serving

Quail
with soy, sesame and celery sauce

Delicate, fine quail marry well with the aromatic eastern flavours in this celery-rich sauce.

Serves 4

method

Bring the water, honey and soy together to a gentle boil, then brush over the quail while the liquid is still hot.

Heat the oil in a frying pan over a medium heat and add all the ingredients for the sauce and simmer for five minutes. Season to taste.

Heat 2 tbsp groundnut or sunflower oil in a non-stick frying pan over a medium to high heat and fry the quail until well browned on each side. Add a good pinch of salt as they cook. When the quail are browned, add the sauce and cook, tossing the quail to coat them in the sauce. Remove from the heat and cut the quail into four portions. Reheat in the simmering sauce for a minute then transfer to a large warmed serving dish.

ingredients

4 quail at room temperature

300ml water

1 tbsp honey

2 tbsp soy sauce

For the sauce:

A little groundnut or sunflower oil

200g celery, peeled and cut into batons

1 tbsp sesame oil

1 tbsp soy

1 tbsp honey

1 tbsp toasted sesame seeds

2 tsp tomato purée

300ml dark chicken stock (see page 31)

Chicken/Guinea fowl drumsticks
with soy, honey, ginger and garlic

More-ish snack food for weekend parties or picnics.

method

Mix all the ingredients together. Marinate the drumsticks in this mixture for four hours.

Preheat the oven to 200C/Gas mark 7. Place the drumsticks on a roasting tin lined with non-stick baking paper and cook for 20 minutes or until the juices run clear when pierced with a sharp knife.

ingredients

6 drumsticks

15g fresh ginger, peeled and finely grated

1 clove garlic, peeled and finely chopped

2 tbsp soy sauce

2 tbsp honey

1 tbsp sherry

1 chopped spring onion top

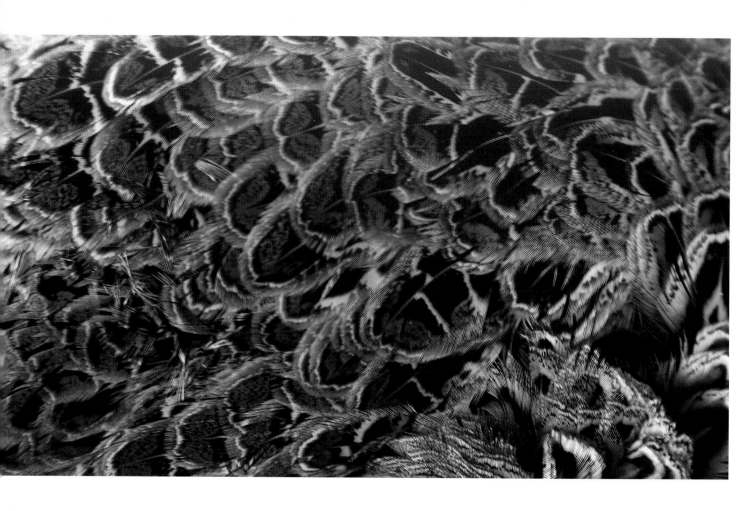

Meat and game

British farmers produce some of the best meat in the world, in high welfare conditions that are second to none. Free range and organically reared animals can be sourced widely now, as can rare breed meat, which has character and provenance. You should always ask your butcher where his or her meat comes from – a local source may well offer a more distinct flavour or character than mass produced meat.

Buying locally also means that you are supporting the local economy. We were lucky at the restaurant to have many good butchers within easy reach and they supplied us daily. In a restaurant, the use of prime cuts is balanced by exploiting less expensive cuts, which benefit from slower cooking to release their flavour and super texture. The recipes in this chapter reflect this with recipes for oxtail as well as beef fillet.

Lowland lamb, delicate and pink, comes to market in late spring and is often roasted, yet here we give a recipe for a poached leg which emphasises the texture and fine flavour of the meat. Free-range pork, too, is a revelation to those used to the dry, characterless, fat-free meat from intensively-reared pigs, and we offer a splendid recipe for a roast loin with cider.

Game is one of the real pleasures of winter and it is pleasing to see that it is now becoming more widely available. It benefits from being hung for several days in a cool, dry place to develop its full flavour, which is remarkable and special. While game birds and tender cuts of venison and hare can be roasted and served pink and moist, the legs and less tender cuts can be minced and made into a delicious game pie which is more than worth the effort to make. Hare, stronger in flavour than its cousin the rabbit, is such a special treat that has an intense flavour unlike anything else – cooking it will fully reward your efforts.

Loin of pork
with prunes and a herb crust

Ask your butcher to remove the skin and bones from the pork, but make sure you get them as they are used in the recipe.

Serves 6

method

Using a small knife, make small incisions in the underside of the meat and stuff with half the prunes. Season the underside well, then truss the loin and place on the bones and skin in a roasting tin with the cider and stock around the meat. Roast in an oven preheated to 220C/Gas mark 7 for an hour and a half, basting occasionally.

Mix together the herbs and breadcrumbs and set aside. Remove the pork from the oven and drain off the juices into a saucepan. Discard the bones and skin. Skim off the fat that rises to the top of the cooking liquid and add it to the breadcrumbs, mixing to combine. Take the string off the pork, place it back in the roasting tin and pack the crumb mixture onto it. Put the tin back in the oven until the crust is golden brown, then remove and keep warm on a serving dish.

Add the remaining prunes to the cooking juices and bring to a simmer over a high heat. When it reaches a boil, reduce the heat to low and cook the prunes for ten minutes so that they soften. Taste the juices and season with salt and pepper to taste.

To serve, carve the pork into thin slices and dress with the prunes and some of the cooking juices spooned over. This is particularly nice served with Parsnip and Apple Gratin (see page 44) or Red Cabbage with Apple and Orange (see page 47).

ingredients

1.8kg piece of loin pork

225g prunes, pitted and halved

1.2 litres medium dry cider

300ml dark chicken or pork stock (see page 31)

4 tbsp chopped fresh herbs (any combination of thyme, rosemary, basil, parsley and marjoram)

225g soft white breadcrumbs

Salt and freshly ground black pepper

Spiced plum sauce

This makes a really good accompaniment to traditional roast pork as an alternative to apple sauce. It can be made in advance and simply warmed through just before serving.

method

Halve and stone the plums and put all the ingredients into a heavy based pan. Cover and simmer gently for about 15 minutes until plums are soft. Remove half of the plums. Take out the star anise from the remaining mixture and liquidise. Add to the cooked plums.

ingredients

450g red plums

1/2 red chilli deseeded and finely chopped

100g caster sugar

100ml white wine vinegar

1 star anise

Bresaola

This recipe involves curing a piece of beef for one week then drying it for a further two weeks. When ready, the beef is sliced thin and eaten raw. It works particularly well as an antipasto or as part of a salad of chicory and sliced radishes. As the meat is hung in a dry place for two weeks after it is cured, be careful to ensure that any flies cannot access it. Hygiene is essential at all times when curing meat. When turning the beef, use vinyl gloves so as not to contaminate it before it is cured.

A dry, cool larder is the best place to hang it so this dish is best made in the cooler months.

method

Mix together all the ingredients except the beef and put in a deep ceramic, stainless steel or plastic dish sterilised with scalding hot water. Submerge the beef in the liquid and leave to marinate for one week in the fridge, turning the beef every day. Hang in a dry place for two weeks then trim off any dry meat around the outside. Rub with olive oil and slice very thinly. Serve with a drizzle of extra virgin olive oil and freshly ground black pepper.

ingredients

425ml light red wine

75ml light white wine

175g coarse sea salt

1 small bunch rosemary

12 cloves

20 black peppercorns

1½ cloves garlic, peeled and crushed

2 strips orange peel

6 dried chillies

½ tsp saltpetre substitute (available from good butchers)

1.15kg topside beef, trimmed of all fat

Extra virgin olive oil and freshly ground black pepper to serve

Rabbit
with thyme and lemon

method

Heat half the butter in a large non-stick frying pan over a high heat, fry the onions whole until brown and put them in a 2-litre casserole. Sprinkle the rabbit with the thyme, flour and a little salt and pepper then fry in the remaining butter until lightly browned. Add to the casserole. Add the stock and wine to the frying pan, bring to the boil, add the lemon juice and zest then check the seasoning and add the liquid to the casserole.

Cover and cook gently in a cool oven, 150C/Gas mark 2, for 45 minutes or until tender. Stir in some cream and mustard, and check the seasoning.

ingredients

25g unsalted butter

16 pickling onions or small shallots, peeled

900g boneless rabbit, cut into large chunks

1 tbsp fresh thyme leaves

1 tbsp plain flour

425ml rabbit or chicken stock (see page 31)

425ml light white wine

Juice and zest of 1 lemon

Salt and freshly ground black pepper

To finish:

100ml double cream

2 tsp Dijon mustard

Venison
with mushrooms, onions and pigs trotters

For this recipe, the venison is first marinated overnight before it is browned and braised with trotters and aromatics, which give a richly flavoured and unctuous result. We like to serve this with a purée of celeriac, made simply by simmering chunks of the peeled vegetable in milk, then blending the drained chunks with a little butter and seasoning to taste.

method

Mix together the red wine, garlic, parsley stalks, thyme and bay leaf, put in a bowl with the venison and marinate overnight.

Next day, heat the dripping in a large casserole and brown the sliced onion and belly pork well, turning them to ensure the pieces of pork and onions are well coloured, then remove from the pan and reserve. Drain and dry the meat, making sure to keep the marinade. Cover the meat with the flour and brown it in the pan of dripping. Add the marinade, the reserved onions and belly pork, and the jellied stock. Tuck in the split trotters and season well. Cover the pan and cook very gently at 150C/Gas mark 2 for about an hour.

Lift the meat and the trotters out of the pan and strain the sauce into a bowl or a jug. Add the mushrooms and the onions to the pan then pour on the sauce and cook for another 15 minutes or until the vegetables are tender. Return the venison to the pan and reheat gently. Check the seasoning and serve piping hot.

ingredients

900g shoulder of venison cut into neat 3cm pieces

For the marinade:

300ml red wine

2 cloves garlic, peeled and chopped

1 small bunch parsley stalks, washed

1 large sprig fresh thyme

1 bay leaf

For finishing the dish:

55g dripping

1 large onion, peeled and sliced

225g salted belly pork, pancetta or streaky bacon cut into lardons

1 tbsp plain flour

150ml jellied chicken or beef stock (see page 31 or 32)

2 pigs trotters, split (ask your butcher to do this for you)

450g pickling onions or small shallots, peeled

225g button mushrooms, wiped

Poached leg of lamb
with caper sauce

This light, delicate dish is an unusual way to cook lamb that will surprise anyone who tries it. The melting texture of the slowly poached lamb marries perfectly with the aromatic capers in the sauce. Some lightly steamed mange tout and asparagus are perfect accompaniments. For this dish, you will need a large pan or deep flameproof casserole for poaching the lamb. Ask your butcher to cut through the shinbone to shorten the leg and tie it into a neat shape so that it cooks evenly.

Serves 8-10

method

Put the lamb into a deep casserole and add the vegetables and herbs. Cover with stock and bring to the boil. Simmer gently for one hour, turning the leg half way through so that it cooks evenly. If you have a temperature probe, the thickest part of the lamb should be no less than 45C before you remove it from the heat. Remove from the pan and leave to rest for at least half an hour. During this time, the heat in the meat will equalize so that the lamb should be cooked through perfectly. An internal temperature of 55C will give lovely pink lamb.

Use a ladle to take out 1.2 litres of stock from the pan then boil it in a large pan over a high heat to reduce it by half.

To make the sauce, place 25g butter in a pan over a medium heat and add the flour once the butter has begun to melt. Cook, stirring for two or three minutes, until the mixture foams and begins to smell nutty. Add the reduced stock little by little, and use a flat whisk to combine the mixture into a smooth sauce. Finish with cream and lemon juice. Season to taste with a little salt and pepper and simmer gently for five minutes over a low heat. Add the chopped capers and the parsley, and season again if required.

To serve, carve the meat into thin slices and dress with the sauce and some freshly cooked vegetables.

ingredients

2.5kg leg of lamb at room temperature, trimmed of any excess fat

2 carrots, peeled

2 onions, peeled

2 pieces celery, washed and trimmed

1 small bunch parsley stalks

1 sprig fresh thyme

2 bay leaves

1 tsp black peppercorns

2 litres lamb or chicken stock (see page 32 or 31)

For the sauce:

25g butter, melted

25g flour

2 tbsp capers, drained

1 tbsp chopped parsley

50ml double cream

Juice of ½ lemon

Salt and freshly ground black pepper

Loin of lamb in filo pastry
with vine leaves and lemon sabayon

At the restaurant, we would buy lamb loins on the bone. We used the bones to make a strong lamb stock, an excellent base for the sauces accompanying any of the lamb dishes on the menu. If buying boned loins of lamb, ask your butcher for the bones and use them to make a strong lamb stock.

Serves 4

method

Remove all the fat and silvery skin from the meat and cut each piece in half. Season each piece with a little salt and pepper and wrap it in two vine leaves. Lay a sheet of filo pastry on the table with one corner pointing towards you. Brush with the melted butter, then lay a wrapped lamb fillet on the pastry, in the middle and near to the point. Fold in the sides of the filo, then roll up to make a neat parcel, rather like a spring roll. Repeat the process with the other three pieces of lamb. Line a roasting tin with non-stick baking paper and put the parcels in, brushing them with any leftover butter. Preheat the oven to 220C/Gas mark 7.

Set the parcels aside while you make the base for the sauce.

Put the shallots and wine in a medium saucepan over a high heat and reduce by half, then put the reduction into a blender with the egg, lemon zest and juice, and a little salt and pepper. Blend well. Put the lamb parcels into the preheated oven for ten minutes, then let them rest for five minutes in a warm place.

Bring the lamb stock to the boil in a saucepan then slowly add it to the blender while the machine is running, which will make a light, frothy sauce. Check the seasoning. If the sauce is not quite thick enough, return it to the pan and cook for a few minutes more, stirring over a very low heat, and finish with a little chopped mint. Cut each parcel in half and serve on top of the sauce.

ingredients

2 best ends of lamb, bones removed and core fillets extracted

8 vine leaves (either fresh or in brine)

4 sheets of filo pastry

55g unsalted butter, melted

Salt and freshly ground black pepper

For the lemon sabayon:

1 shallot, peeled and finely chopped

50ml light white wine

1 medium egg

Zest of ½ lemon, grated

Juice of ½ lemon

175ml strong lamb stock (see page 32)

Salt and freshly ground black pepper

1 tbsp chopped fresh mint to serve

Lamb sweetbreads
with vegetables, sorrel and cream

At the restaurant we used to serve this mixture in puff pastry cases, made earlier in the day and then gently warmed through, rather like a giant vol-au-vent. If you have no pastry to hand, they can just as easily be served on toast or with some plain boiled rice – either way they are delicious. We usually soaked the sweetbreads overnight before preparing them for the final cooking.

method

First, prepare the sweetbreads. Put them in a bowl of cold water and leave overnight to remove the blood. Drain the sweetbreads and put them in a pan, add a little lemon juice and salt, then cover with the chicken stock. Bring to the boil and simmer gently for 15 minutes. Leave the sweetbreads to cool in the stock, then drain. When cool, trim off any fat or sinew and either chill in the fridge or finish the dish straight away.

Cook the vegetables lightly in half the butter. Season the sweetbreads with salt, pepper and lemon juice. Fry gently in the remaining butter to brown them lightly, and when you turn them, add the vegetables and the sorrel, or a little chopped tarragon if you prefer. Cook together for a minute or two to heat through then finish with the cream. Check the seasoning and serve immediately.

ingredients

450g lamb sweetbreads

150ml chicken stock (see page 31)

Juice of ½ lemon

115g carrots, peeled and finely diced

115g leeks, washed and finely diced

115g celery or celeriac, finely diced

1 small bunch sorrel, shredded

25g unsalted butter

150ml double cream

Salt and freshly ground black pepper

Raised game pie

A properly made game pie is a splendid thing, well worth the effort. Any mixture of minced game can be used, but the legs of pheasants and wild duck will need any sinews removed before the meat is minced (you may find your butcher can do this for you). Make the pies three or four days in advance, and freeze one for later – it is always worth making two while you can.

method

Heat the butter in a saucepan over a medium heat. Add the shallots and cook, stirring occasionally for five minutes until they are softened but not coloured. Add the Madeira, brandy and port and reduce until the pan is almost dry, then remove from the heat and leave to cool. Mix the pork, fat, shallot reduction and minced game together. Add the chopped parsley, garlic, thyme, quatre épices and salt. Slice the breasts and add to the mixture, making sure to mix together well. Set aside in a cool place while you make the pastry.

To make the pastry, put the salt and flour in a bowl, then put the water and lard in a large saucepan over a high heat and bring to the boil. Pour the liquid onto the flour, mixing well with a wooden spoon, to form a smooth, even dough.

While the pastry is cooling, line two large loaf tins each with a long strip of non-stick baking paper. On a floured surface, divide the pastry into three and roll out two of the pieces to line the tins, allowing a little overlap all the way round. Divide the filling between the two tins, pressing it firmly into the corners. Roll out the remaining pastry, divide it in two and cover the pies, crimping the edges together really well. Make a hole in the middle of both pie tops and brush generously with beaten egg.

Bake in an oven preheated to 190C/Gas mark 5 for two hours. Check that the pies are cooked by piercing with a skewer in the middle. If the juices run clear then the pie is done, if the juices are pink, lower the temperature, cover the top with tin foil and cook for another half an hour.

Remove from the oven and allow the pies to cool to room temperature. Warm the jellied stock gently to liquefy it, then pour half into each pie using a small funnel. If you are using stock and need to add gelatine to set it, simply soak the sheets of gelatine in cold water for ten minutes. Squeeze out the gelatine and add to half the stock in a small pan. Warm the stock over a low heat to melt the gelatine, then add the remaining stock and cool to room temperature before pouring into the pies. Allow the pies to chill in the fridge, in their tins, for at least 24 hours before removing them. They will benefit from being kept three or four days before eating.

ingredients

Makes 2 large loaf-sized pies

15g unsalted butter

4 shallots, peeled and chopped

100ml Madeira

100ml brandy

100ml port

300g fat belly pork mince

150g streaky bacon, finely chopped

75g pork back fat, finely chopped

1kg mixed minced game

1 bunch parsley

1 clove garlic

1 sprig thyme

1 tsp quatre épices

2 tsp salt

700g skinned game breasts

For the pastry:

900g plain flour1 tsp salt

250g lard

250ml water

1 egg, lightly beaten, to glaze

For the jelly:

500ml jellied game stock, or 500ml strong game stock and 4 sheets gelatine (see page 32)

Braised partridge
with cabbage, sausage and bacon

You will rarely come across older partridges unless you shoot, in which case you may want to extend the cooking time a little. Young partridges will cook very quickly indeed, and can be served slightly pink to keep them moist and tender.

method

Season the birds with a little salt and pepper and a sprig of thyme inside. Heat a little dripping in a large non-stick frying pan or skillet over a medium high heat, add the partridges and fry to brown them all over, then transfer to a flameproof casserole. Put the sausages and bacon in the pan, stirring until they begin to brown, then add to the birds in the casserole. Add the herbs, stock, wine and seasoning, bring the casserole to a gentle simmer, then cover and reduce the heat to low.

Cook for 15-20 minutes, depending on the age of the birds, until they are almost cooked. You can tell by piercing the thickest part of the breast with a sharp knife: if the juices run clear, and the breasts feel firm, the birds are cooked.

Transfer the birds to a warm plate and add the cabbage to the casserole on a medium heat. Cook the cabbage until it is tender, then return the birds to the cabbage, nestling them in to warm through for a few minutes. Serve immediately.

ingredients

4 partridges, trussed

1 tbsp dripping

8 chipolata sausages

115g unsmoked streaky bacon, sliced

1 bay leaf

1 large sprig fresh thyme

150ml chicken stock (see page 31)

150ml Riesling or other white wine

450g prepared Savoy cabbage

Salt and freshly ground black pepper

Roast partridge
with grapes, brandy and cream

method

Preheat the oven to 200C/Gas mark 6.

Season the cavities of the birds with a little salt and pepper, a sprig of thyme and a knob of butter. Heat the remaining butter in a large non-stick frying pan or skillet over a medium high heat. Brown the partridges well on all sides, then transfer to a small roasting tin. Cook in the oven for ten minutes.

Remove the birds from the oven and place the roasting tin on the stove. Add the brandy and carefully set the fumes alight with a match to burn off the alcohol. Transfer the birds to a warm plate and set the roasting tin over a medium heat. Add the chicken stock and bring to a simmer, then add the cream and keep simmering while stirring to combine. Season to taste, then strain the sauce into a clean pan. Bring back up to a simmer and add the grapes.

To serve, carve the legs from the birds and remove the breasts. Serve on warm plates with the sauce spooned over and some watercress and game chips on the side.

ingredients

4 young partridges

40g unsalted butter

4 sprigs fresh thyme

1 small glass brandy

150ml chicken stock (see page 31)

225ml double cream

225g white grapes, halved and pipped

Watercress and game chips to serve

Spiced lamb patties

method

If the lamb is not already minced, mix it with the rest of the ingredients except the yoghurt and put it through the mincer. Once minced, add the yoghurt and mix well. If the lamb is already minced then combine all the ingredients and mix well. Shape the meat into small patties, each weighing about 55g.

In a frying pan, sweat the onions and garlic in some olive oil, add the ginger, yoghurt, tomatoes, a little water and some salt and pepper, and cook for about five minutes. Place the patties carefully in the pan with the sauce, then cover and cook in a cool oven for about 25 minutes.

Remove the patties from the pan and keep warm while you reduce the sauce on the stove. Serve the patties and sauce with rice, yoghurt and a generous sprinkling of dukkah.

ingredients

450g trimmed or minced lamb

½ tsp ground cumin

½ tsp ground coriander

½ tsp salt

½ tsp garam masala

1 good pinch cayenne

1 small bunch fresh coriander

2 tbsp plain yoghurt

For the sauce:

115g onion, chopped

1 clove garlic, peeled and chopped

Olive oil

1 inch piece fresh root ginger, grated

150ml yoghurt

250g tinned plum tomatoes

Water

Salt and freshly ground black pepper

Dukkah

This traditional Egyptian spice mix is a super accompaniment to lamb patties.

method

Lightly roast all the ingredients in a dry frying pan then pound in a mortar or blend carefully in a coffee grinder. Any left over can be stored in a jar in a larder for up to a month.

ingredients

125g sesame seeds

60g coriander seeds

30g skinned hazelnuts

30g cumin seed

Fillet of beef
with peperonata

Serves 4

method

Allow the beef to come up to room temperature, covered, for a couple of hours. Preheat the oven to 180C/Gas mark 4.

Heat a large frying pan or skillet on a high heat, and add the sunflower oil and butter. When it sizzles, add the beef and sprinkle with a little salt and black pepper. Let the beef brown well on its underside, then turn it carefully with a pair of tongs and allow it to brown really well all over. Remove from the heat and place the beef in a roasting tin. Sprinkle over the shallots and thyme and roll the beef so that they coat the fillet.

Place the tin in the oven and cook for 20 minutes, or until the meat feels just firm to the touch and a temperature probe inserted to its thickest part registers 45C for a medium rare result. Remove the beef from the oven and place it on a heated serving plate, reserving the tin and all its juices and caramelised bits for the peperonata. Cover the fillet with foil and leave to rest in a warm place for 20 minutes. During this time, the internal temperature will increase by as much as 10C, and the juices will equalise throughout the meat.

Garnish with fresh basil and serve sliced on a plate with peperonata (see below).

ingredients

1kg fillet of beef, centre cut, trimmed of silver skin and sinew

25g unsalted butter

2 tbsp sunflower oil

Salt and freshly ground black pepper

2 shallots, peeled and finely chopped

1 large sprig fresh thyme

Peperonata

This is an excellent accompaniment to fillet of beef.

method

Sweat the onion and garlic in the olive oil in a pan over a medium heat for about five minutes. Add the pepper, mixing in well. Reduce the heat, then cover and cook for another five minutes until the pepper is tender. Add the tomatoes, season, and cook until reduced and thickened. Finish by scattering some torn basil leaves. When ready to serve, reheat in the roasting tin used for the fillet of beef.

ingredients

1 large red pepper, seeded and sliced

1 onion, peeled and sliced

2 cloves garlic, finely chopped

15 ml olive oil

1 tin peeled and chopped plum tomatoes

1 small bunch fresh basil leaves, torn

Beef with Burgundy

Serves 6-8

method

Lay the beef in a shallow dish and cover with the red wine, sliced onions, thyme, parsley and bay leaf. Drizzle over the olive oil and leave to marinate overnight.

Dice the bacon, then heat the dripping in a large ovenproof casserole over a medium high heat and add the bacon pieces, and the rind if you have it. Allow the bacon to sizzle and when it begins to brown, add the onions. Fry the onions and bacon together, stirring occasionally, until the onions are browned. Remove the vegetables and bacon with a slotted spoon and reserve, then remove the pan from the stove.

Lift the beef from the marinade and dry on kitchen paper, taking care to reserve the marinade. Place the meat on a board in a single layer and scatter over some of the flour, then turn the pieces and sprinkle the remaining flour. Return the pan to a high heat and brown the beef, adding a pinch of salt and black pepper to the pieces as they cook. Turn frequently so that all the chunks are well browned on both sides. Add the marinade, stock and garlic and bring to the boil, then remove from the heat and cover the casserole.

Place in an oven preheated to 140C/Gas mark 1-2 and cook for half an hour, then reduce the heat to 120C/Gas mark 1 and cook for a further one and a half or two hours until the meat is very tender. Add the onion and bacon mixture and the mushrooms, and cook for a further 20 minutes. Remove from the oven, taste for seasoning and remove the whole herbs. Serve immediately, or allow the casserole to cool and either chill for up to two days or freeze for later use.

ingredients

1 kg chuck steak, trimmed of excess fat and cut into 1cm chunks

250ml red Burgundy

1 large onion, peeled and sliced

1 sprig fresh thyme

1 sprig fresh parsley

1 bay leaf

30ml olive oil

120g thickly sliced streaky bacon or lardons, rind removed but reserved

2 tbsp dripping

2 tbsp plain flour

16 small shallots or pickling onions, peeled, root plate left intact

250ml beef stock (see page 32)

2 cloves garlic, peeled and chopped

16 button mushrooms

Salt and freshly ground black pepper

Roast pheasant

Serves 4-6

method

Rinse the insides of the pheasants and check that all the internal organs have been removed. Pat the pheasants dry on kitchen paper. Preheat the oven to 220C/Gas mark 7.

Place a large frying pan on a high heat and add the oil and 25g butter. When it sizzles, add the birds and brown them well all over. When brown, remove them from the heat and transfer to a large roasting tin, leaving plenty of space around each bird. Divide the butter and shallots between the cavities and season the birds both inside and out with a little salt and black pepper. Roast the birds for 30-35 minutes or until a skewer inserted to the breast just above the wing produces clear liquid and the birds feel firm. It is important not to overcook them as they will be dry.

Remove the birds from the oven and allow them to rest in a warm place for between 15 and 30 minutes. Drain any juices from the roasting tin into a small pan and bring to a simmer over a medium heat. Add the pomegranate molasses and taste. The juices should be light, sharp and slightly sweet. Correct the seasoning and keep warm. Cut the legs from the birds and remove the breasts whole, carving them into long pieces. Divide the meat between warmed serving plates and drizzle over the juices. Serve with Saffron Pilaf (see page 57).

ingredients

2 pheasants, preferably hens, at room temperature

25g unsalted butter for frying

1 tbsp sunflower oil

2 tbsp unsalted butter for stuffing

2 shallots, peeled and finely chopped

½ tsp ground cinnamon

2 tbsp pomegranate molasses

Salt and freshly ground black pepper

Saddle of hare
baked in cream

This recipe comes from Lucien Tendret via Elizabeth David's *French Provincial Cooking* – one of the most influential books ever published. Hare is special, a real treat. You should choose your dining companion, and wine, carefully when making this lovely dish. A good Rhône marries well with the rich, flavourful meat and sauce.

Serves 2

method

First, trim the silver skin from the hare: using a small sharp knife, nick the silver membrane that covers the surface of the saddle. Run your knife under the tough membrane, cutting closely to it, to remove all the membrane from the surface of the meat in strips. Additionally, trim any membrane that is loose around the edge of the saddle. Set the hare aside, covered, to come up to room temperature.

When you are ready to cook, preheat the oven to 140C/Gas mark 1.

Place the saddle in a long, narrow dish or terrine that is just large enough to hold it. Add the shallots, cream and red wine vinegar and a pinch of salt. Cover the dish with a lid or a piece of foil and place it in the oven for 45 minutes.

Remove, uncover and taste for seasoning, adding a little salt and black pepper to taste. Replace in the oven for a further 15 minutes, uncovered, and then transfer the hare to a warm serving dish and place the sauce in a wide saucepan over a medium to high heat. Bring the sauce to a simmer, and reduce slightly, adding the redcurrant jelly, whisking to amalgamate. Remove the sauce from the heat.

Carve the saddle into long strips, cutting either side of the backbone. Serve on heated plates with the sauce poured over. As Elizabeth David suggests, a dish of chestnuts or celeriac purée goes very well with this.

ingredients

1 saddle of young hare, on the bone

2 large shallots, peeled and finely diced

250ml double cream

2 tbsp red wine vinegar

2 tsp redcurrant jelly

Salt and freshly ground black pepper

Oxtail *with grapes*

This recipe comes from Elizabeth David's *French Provincial Cooking*, and is just super. We have lost touch with the seasons today, but traditionally in October in some wine producing regions, the end of the crop was left on the vines for local people to cook or dry for winter stores. This dish marries such fruit with oxtail, another traditional and inexpensive ingredient, and the result is a classic of French cooking. Muscat-scented Italia grapes work well if you can find them.

Serves 6-8

method

Place a large casserole on a medium heat and add the dripping. When it has melted, add the bacon. Fry, stirring occasionally until the bacon fat renders and the pieces are lightly browned. Add the onions, carrots and oxtail pieces and cook for two or three minutes, then add the garlic, thyme, bay and sage. Add a pinch of salt and pepper, and cook together for a further two to three minutes on a low heat. Gently crush 800g of the grapes in a large bowl and add to the pan along with the mace.

Preheat the oven to 140C/Gas mark 1.

Bring the pan to a simmer, then cover and place in the preheated oven. Cook for four to five hours until the meat is very tender and almost falling from the bones. While the meat is cooking, cut the remaining grapes in half.

When the meat is tender, remove the pieces from the casserole and set aside. Purée the sauce in a liquidizer, then sieve into a clean pan over a low to medium heat. Bring the sauce to a gentle simmer and taste for seasoning. Simmer the sauce a little longer if it seems too light or thin. Then place the oxtail pieces back in the sauce and reheat. Add the halved grapes and serve.

ingredients

2 tbsp dripping or lard

225g diced streaky bacon or lardons

4 large onions, peeled and diced

2 large carrots, washed and sliced

2 oxtails, sliced into sections and trimmed of excess fat

4 cloves or garlic, peeled and roughly chopped

1 sprig fresh thyme

1 bay leaf

1 fresh sage leaf

1kg seedless grapes, stripped from their stalks

1 pinch ground mace

Salt and freshly ground black pepper

111

Bakery

Good butter and flour are essential for good quality baking, as are good eggs. There is a seemingly endless variety of biscuits and cakes in our repertoire and we are always keen to try new recipes and combinations. Having said that, there is little more comforting than a simple fruit tart or a crisp langue de chat where the flavour of the simple raw materials comes to the fore.

Bread making has, it seems, made a resurgence in homes across the land as people begin to appreciate how easy it is to make good quality bread at home, far better than most supermarkets churn out. At the restaurant we made bread in variety, and were regularly inspired to experiment with sourdoughs and unusual recipes by our friend Tom Jaine who worked at the restaurant as Joyce's partner for a decade.

British companies, like Marriages based in Essex, are now producing good quality, home-grown bread flours in many varieties and are well worth searching out in your local shops. We tend to use fresh yeast for baking which is less widely available than it used to be. As a substitute you could use Dove's Farm organic yeast or Fermipan, which both give excellent results.

Baking demands care and attention, and it is worth investing in a set of digital scales that give accurate measurements. They are especially useful when measuring small amounts of liquid (remember that 1ml water equals 1g).

Sweet pastry

This sweet pastry comes from Roger Vergé, and is superb. It is tricky to handle, but as long as you keep your pastry cold you will find it works well. Make a batch and then cut into pieces of roughly 200g which will be sufficient to roll out to a 20cm tart shell. A pinch of baking powder added to the pastry makes it less likely to collapse in the oven.

method

Beat the butter together with the icing sugar in a large bowl. Add the lemon zest, rum, egg and yolks, beat again, then sieve in the flour, salt and baking powder if used. Mix together until the pastry is a smooth, evenly-mixed mass. Do not worry if the pastry is very soft as it will firm up in the fridge. Simply pile the pastry into 200g pieces on sheets of cling film, then wrap and form into a flattened round. Chill for 30 minutes, remove and knead each lightly then replace in the fridge. This makes the pastry chill evenly. It can be then used immediately or frozen for up to one month. To use, remove the pastry from the fridge and allow it to rest at room temperature for ten minutes. Remove the cling film, knead the pastry lightly to make it malleable, and then roll out on a well-floured surface, or between two floured sheets of non-stick baking paper, to your desired size.

ingredients

500g fine plain flour

375g unsalted butter, at warm room temperature

150g icing sugar

45ml white rum

1 whole egg

2 egg yolks

100g ground almonds

Zest of one lemon

Pinch of salt

Pinch of baking powder (optional)

Shortcrust pastry

This enriched pastry is used for Salmon in pastry (see page 68), but it can also be used to line the sweet tarts in the book – it is easier to handle than the sweet pastry and is perfect for beginners.

method

Place the flour, cubed butter and salt in a food processor and blitz until the mixture resembles fine breadcrumbs. Tip into a bowl and make a well in the centre. In a separate small bowl, beat the egg together with the lemon juice and add it to the well. Using a large table fork mix the pastry together, working quickly. Fully incorporate the egg until the mixture is evenly hydrated and there are no dry or wet lumps. At this stage you should be able to pinch the pastry together with your fingertips – if not, add a little cold water and mix again. Shape the pastry into a ball and form into a flattened round. Wrap in cling film and allow the pastry to rest in the fridge for at least 30 minutes before using.

ingredients

150g plain flour

90g unsalted butter, chilled

1 good pinch salt

1 egg, chilled

½ tsp lemon juice

Water to mix

Puff pastry

Home-made puff pastry has a marvellous butteryness that is lacking in commercial products. But the process is time consuming, so it makes sense to prepare a big batch and freeze what you are not going to use straight away.

Makes 8 pie crusts

method

Sift the flour and salt into a bowl or into a mixer with a dough hook. Rub in 100g of the butter. Make a well in the centre and pour in the lemon juice and enough cold water to form a dough (you'll need about 600ml). Cover and leave to rest in the fridge for half an hour.

Divide the remaining butter in two. Put each half between two sheets of grease-proof paper and use a rolling pin to flatten each one into a slab about 20cm square. Peel off the paper, sprinkle the butter with a little flour, wrap in fresh paper and chill until the butter is firm.

On a lightly floured surface, roll out the dough into a rectangle roughly 60x20cm. Lay the two slabs of butter side-by-side over two-thirds of the pastry. Flip the uncovered third over the butter, then fold the buttered pastry on top of the first flap. Give the pastry a quarter turn so the folded edge is facing you and roll out again to a 60x20cm rectangle. Make another quarter turn and roll again.

Rolling puff pastry requires some technique: give the dough short, sharp rolls, and avoid pushing the rolling pin along the dough as this tends to push out the butter. When you have turned and rolled twice, fold in three and leave to rest for another half an hour in the fridge.

Repeat the turning, rolling and folding twice more so you have rolled six times in all. The butter should no longer be visible: if the dough appears streaky, give it another roll and turn. Divide into eight slabs, wrap well and freeze until needed.

ingredients

900g flour
2 tsp salt
900g butter, chilled
Juice of ½ lemon

Langues de chat

These delicate biscuits are versatile and can be served with ice creams or summer berries. You will see we recommend you weigh the egg white: when measuring small volumes of liquid, it is often easier to get accurate measurements by weight.

method

Preheat the oven to 180C/Gas mark 4.

Place the butter in a large bowl and beat with a wooden spoon to lighten it. Add the caster sugar and beat until the mixture is light and fluffy. Add the egg white in two or three batches, beating well with each addition. If at any time the mixture separates, place the bowl over another containing hot water and stir to amalgamate. Remove from the hot water and beat in the remaining egg. Then, using a metal spoon or spatula, fold in the sieved flour until you have an even mixture. The mixture can now be cooked immediately.

Line several baking trays with non-stick baking paper and fit a piping bag with a plain 5mm nozzle. Pipe several evenly-spaced lines of the mixture about 10cm long. Space the biscuits at least 4cm apart as they do tend to spread as they bake.

Bake the biscuits for ten minutes or so until they are evenly browned around the edges and still a little pale in the middle. When the biscuits are cooked, remove them to a wire rack, carefully lifting them from the tray with a palette knife. When they are completely cool, store in an airtight tin.

ingredients

115g caster sugar

115g unsalted butter at room temperature

115g plain flour, sieved

125g egg white, lightly beaten

tip

If you like, you can mix a tablespoon of the mixture with ½ tsp cocoa powder until smooth, place this into a small piping bag and use to decorate the biscuits before they are baked. Expert pipers might like to try writing the names of their dinner guests along each biscuit before they are baked.

Gingerbread biscuits

These delightful biscuits complement a dish of poached rhubarb served with thick cream, but they can equally be baked into fancy shapes for your Christmas tree – iced and decorated they are very pretty.

method

Preheat the oven to 170C/Gas mark 3.

Place the treacle and syrup in a medium saucepan over a low heat until liquid, then remove from the heat and add the remaining ingredients. Mix well with a wooden spoon until smooth then transfer to a lightly floured surface. Using a rolling pin, roll out to about 5mm thick. Cut into your desired shapes – small rounds or suchlike – and transfer the biscuits to baking trays lined with non-stick baking paper. Bake in the oven for 20 minutes. The biscuits will brown lightly but will still be soft when baked – they crisp as they cool. Remove from the oven when they are firm and transfer to a wire rack until thoroughly cool.

ingredients

450g plain flour

250g unsalted butter

225g caster sugar

2 heaped tsp ground ginger

115g black treacle or molasses

115g golden syrup or honey

Palmiers

These biscuits are made with puff pastry or pastry trimmings rolled
out with lots of icing sugar, then folded so that when they cook, they
expand into rounded heart-shaped, crisp, caramelised biscuits that
we used to serve with coffee or ice creams. If you have puff pastry
trimmings from another recipe, it is worth making the palmiers and then
freezing the rolls so that you have them ready in the freezer for when
you need them. The rolls can then be slightly defrosted before slicing
and cooking.

ingredients

250g puff pastry
70g icing sugar

method

Preheat the oven to 220C/Gas mark 7.

Sprinkle your work surface and the puff pastry with icing sugar and roll
it out to a 30x20cm rectangle, using icing sugar as you would flour to
roll out pastry. Mark the centre of the rolled out pastry lengthways with
the back of a knife. Now fold each edge into the centreline, and then
fold the length in half again, trapping the edges in the centre of the fold.

Leave to rest in the fridge for 30 minutes and then slice thinly into
2-3mm slices and place on baking trays lined with non-stick baking
paper, sprinkling a little additional icing sugar onto each biscuit. Space
the biscuits well apart as they expand substantially in the oven.

Place in the oven for 5-10 minutes until they are lightly browned, then
flip the biscuits over and cook for a further five minutes until they are
evenly browned and crisp. Transfer to a wire rack until cool. Best
eaten as soon as possible but can be stored in an airtight tin.

Focaccia

This recipe is based on the one in Tom Jaine's book, *'Making Bread at Home'*. Tom was a partner at the restaurant when we opened and contributed a number of recipes over the years. This bread is a fine accompaniment to salads and summer foods – it is great for mopping up the juices of ripe tomatoes. When sliced and toasted, it can be used for making bruschetta and canapés.

method

Dissolve the yeast in the water in a mixing jug and combine it with the wine, flour and salt to make a dough. Mix vigorously until the dough is elastic and smooth, then add the olive oil and mix again until the oil is incorporated. Transfer the dough to a floured work surface. Knead the dough for ten minutes then leave to rise, covered with oiled cling film, for one and a half hours or until doubled in size.

Shape the dough into a flat disc about 25cm in diameter. Line a roasting tin with non-stick baking paper and transfer the dough to it. Again cover with oiled cling film and put in a warm place for 30 minutes. Dimple the focaccia with your fingertips, pressing nearly to the bottom of the dough. Cover with oiled cling film and leave for another two hours.

Preheat the oven to 220C/Gas mark 7.

Scatter the surface of the loaf with the sea salt crystals and drizzle a little oil in the dimples. Bake for 20-25 minutes. The bread is cooked when the surface is evenly browned and sounds hollow when tapped. Cool on a wire rack.

ingredients

15g fresh yeast

150ml lukewarm water

30ml dry light white wine

280g unbleached white bread flour

1 tsp salt

1 tbsp extra virgin olive oil

Sea salt crystals and additional extra virgin olive oil for topping

Buttermilk rolls

Another recipe from Tom Jaine, this makes a soft, sweet milky dough that is baked as small folded rolls that pull apart easily. We used to make them for Sunday lunches when, generally, diners spent a little more time with us, enjoying the effort we put into the food. Buttermilk can be sourced in health food shops and some supermarkets. If you can't find it, a good alternative is a mixture of half yogurt, half water.

method

Crumble the yeast into the liquid. Mix in the honey and leave to ferment for 30 minutes in a warm place. Melt half the butter. Sift the flour and bicarbonate of soda together and put into the bowl of a food mixer. Add the honey liquid and the melted butter and mix for eight minutes, making sure that all the flour is mixed in thoroughly. Cover the bowl and put in a warm place for one hour or until the dough has doubled in volume.

Tip the dough onto a floured surface and knead to form a smooth ball. Divide the dough into three and roll each piece carefully into a rectangle about 25x30cm. Melt the remaining butter and brush each rectangle, then stack them on top of each other. Cut the rectangle into six strips lengthways and put them on top of each other in pairs so that you have three strips, each six layers high. Now cut each strip into six squares, making 18 squares in all, and pinch one side of each square. Butter 18 small patty pans or deep muffin tins, and place a stack of dough, pinch side down, in each hole. Cover the rolls with greased cling film or a slightly damp cloth, and allow the rolls to rise in a warm place for one hour.

Bake in an oven preheated to 220C/Gas mark 7 for 15 minutes. The rolls are cooked when they are evenly browned and sound hollow when tapped.

ingredients

525g white flour

20g fresh yeast, or 1 tsp active dried yeast

375ml cultured buttermilk, or half yoghurt half water

85g butter

20g honey

1 tsp bicarbonate of soda

1¼ tsp salt

Hot cross buns

We used to make these lovely buns each year, starting on Maundy Thursday, allowing the buns to rise slowly overnight to give the yeast time to work in the rich, spicy dough. Come Good Friday, a large basket of them would be placed in the restaurant for our suppliers and customers to help themselves.

method

Mix the yeast into the milk and stir to combine. Put all the ingredients but the dried fruit into a mixer to knead for ten minutes, adding the fruit at the end. Put the dough into a floured bowl, cover with a damp cloth and leave to rise at room temperature for two hours. Divide the dough into 25 pieces and shape into buns. Put the buns onto a greased baking tray, cover with a damp tea towel and leave to rise for one hour or until doubled in size. Alternatively the rolls can be left in a cool place overnight.

While the buns are rising, preheat the oven to 220C/Gas mark 7. Mix together 115g of flour and 1 tbsp of oil with enough water to make a thick paste. When the buns have doubled in size, pipe on a cross with the flour paste. Bake in a hot oven for 20-30 minutes until golden brown. The rolls are cooked when they are evenly browned and sound hollow when tapped.

When the buns come out of the oven, brush them with 3tbsp of caster sugar dissolved in 3tbsp of milk to glaze.

Elizabeth David's recipe for bun spice

2 tsp nutmeg 3 tsp allspice or ground white peppercorns 1 tsp cinnamon 1 tsp ground cloves 1 tsp ground ginger Good pinch of ground cumin.

method

Mix the spices well in a small bowl and store in an airtight jar until ready to use.

ingredients

500g plain flour

25g fresh yeast

150g currants or sultanas

¼ tsp salt

200ml milk

55g brown sugar

55g butter

2 tsp bun spice (see Elizabeth David's Bun Spice)

2 eggs, beaten

For the cross paste:

115g plain flour

1 tbsp sunflower oil

Water to mix

For the glaze:

3 tbsp caster sugar

3 tbsp milk

Lemon Pernod cake

This moist, citrus scented cake has a light anise flavour from the Pernod. You can, of course, use another liqueur should you prefer, for example, Cointreau or Grand Marnier.

Served for tea with raspberry or rhubarb compote on the side, it is delicious.

method

Lightly grease a 23cm deep round cake tin with butter and line with non-stick baking paper.

In a large bowl, beat together the butter, sugar and lemon zest until the mixture is pale and fluffy. Gradually beat in the eggs, making sure that you mix well all the time until the mixture is glossy and smooth. If the mixture curdles or becomes liquid at any time, simply add a spoonful of flour and continue until all the egg is mixed in.

Fold in the flour and 1 tbsp of the lemon juice mixing lightly but thoroughly. Put into the tin and smooth the top of the cake with the spatula. Bake in an oven preheated to 170C/Gas mark 3 for 20-25 minutes until the cake is evenly browned and a skewer inserted into the centre comes out cleanly.

While the cake is cooking, prepare the syrup by dissolving the sugar in the remaining lemon juice. Add the water and bring the mixture to the boil. Remove from the heat and add the Pernod. When the cake is out of the oven, allow to cool slightly, then pour the syrup over and leave to cool in the tin. When the cake is completely cool, lift it out and store in an airtight tin for up to one week.

ingredients

For the cake:

115g unsalted butter at room temperature

115g caster sugar

115g self-raising flour

Zest and juice of 1 lemon

2 eggs at room temperature, beaten

For the syrup:

85g caster sugar

30ml Pernod

40ml water

Juice of 1½ lemons

Oatmeal and pecan biscuits

These nutty, full-flavoured biscuits are perfect for a morning snack or for tea time, being just sweet enough. Walnuts can be substituted for the pecans but, as with all nuts, make sure they are fresh. Keep nuts in a cool place if you have to store them for any length of time.

method

In a food processor, mix together the sugars and the butter until pale and fluffy. Add the beaten eggs, milk and vanilla, and mix well. Sift in the flour, bicarbonate of soda, baking powder and salt and mix again, pulsing the mixture until it is just bound together. Finally pulse in the oats and nuts. Remove the dough to a sheet of cling film spread out on your work surface and roll into a sausage about 7cm in diameter. Chill in the fridge for at least one hour or until firm enough to slice.

Preheat the oven to 180C/Gas mark 4 and line several baking trays with non-stick baking paper. Remove the cling film and slice the dough into discs. Place the biscuits on a lined baking tray and bake in the oven for 8-10 minutes until they are lightly browned and firm. Transfer the biscuits to a wire rack to cool and store them in an airtight container.

ingredients

225g unsalted butter

175g caster sugar

175g soft brown sugar, sieved if lumpy

2 eggs at room temperature

50ml milk

Seeds from one vanilla pod

250g plain flour

1 tsp bicarbonate of soda

1 tsp baking powder

½ tsp salt

250g pecan nuts, finely chopped

125g rolled oats

Orange sablés

Makes about 25

method

Place the butter, icing sugar, flour, egg yolk and orange zest in a food processor and mix until it resembles breadcrumbs. (Alternatively, you can rub the mixture together with your fingertips.) Add the orange juice to bind the mixture together and knead it lightly into a smooth, even mass. Place the mixture on a sheet of cling film and roll into a sausage about 5cm in diameter. Refrigerate for at least four hours.

To cook, remove the cling film, slice the roll into discs about 5mm thick, and place on a baking tray lined with non-stick baking paper. Cook at 160-170C/Gas mark 3-4 for 5-10 minutes until golden brown all over. Transfer to a wire rack to cool, then store in an airtight tin.

ingredients

140g unsalted butter

85g icing sugar

200g plain flour

3 egg yolks

Zest of 1½ oranges

1 tbsp orange juice

Bombolini

This recipe for lemon scented doughnuts came to us from Nick Coiley who enjoyed making them for Sunday elevenses. Sunday was the one day we didn't stop for staff lunch because diners always seemed to want to book early and stay late. We were then able to enjoy a late lunch ourselves, ready for our evening off!

method

Tip the flour onto a clean work surface, add 30g of the caster sugar, the lemon zest and the salt. Shape it into a mound and make a well in the middle.

Cut the butter into small pieces and put in the middle of the well. Knead the dry ingredients and the butter for about five minutes, adding just enough warm water to combine the ingredients. Crumble the yeast into a teacup and add enough warm water – about 175ml – to make a runny, smooth paste. Add this to the dough and knead for a further 15 minutes or until the dough is completely elastic: it should be soft but not sticky, so add more water or flour if necessary. Put the dough into a lightly floured bowl and cover it with a tea towel and leave to rise in a warm place for one hour.

Tip the dough onto a floured work surface and knead for a couple of minutes before rolling out gently to a thickness of about 1cm. Using a pastry cutter, cut the dough into circles. Lay large napkins or tea towels on two large trays and place the circles on the cloth without touching one another. Re-knead the remaining dough, roll out and cut into circles. Cover them with a cloth and leave to rise in a warm place for one hour.

Heat the oil to 180C in a deep fat fryer or other suitable pan that is deeper than it is wide (the doughnuts must be able to move around freely). If you are using a pan, do not have the oil deeper than one third of the pan.

It is important that the oil is kept at the right temperature, so use a temperature probe to check, and do not leave the pan unattended even just for a minute. When the oil is hot enough, put the doughnuts in two or three at a time. Put the side of the doughnut touching the towel in first, and when that side is cooked turn them over and cook the other side, making sure that the doughnuts are puffed and golden on both sides.

When the doughnuts are cooked, remove them from the oil with a slotted spoon and drain them on kitchen paper. Roll the doughnuts in the remaining sugar and serve warm.

ingredients

450g plain flour

115g caster sugar

Zest of 1 lemon

½ tsp salt

75g unsalted butter, softened

15g fresh yeast

1.2 litres groundnut or sunflower oil, for deep frying

North Staffordshire oatcakes

These soft, flexible oatcakes are made from a batter and are similar to pikelets. Nutty and slightly sweet, they make a lovely accompaniment to smoked fish such as eel or salmon. Serve them with soured cream and perhaps a beetroot salad on the side.

method

Mix together the water and a little of the milk with the yeast. Stir in the sugar and set aside in a warm place for 15 minutes or until frothy.

Sieve the flours into a warmed bowl and stir in the oatmeal. Add the remaining milk to the yeast mixture, make a well in the middle of the dry ingredients and pour in some of the liquid. Gradually mix in the liquid, adding a bit at a time until it is all combined and the mixture has no lumps. Cover the bowl with a damp cloth and set aside in a warm place for one hour for the mixture to rise.

When you are ready to cook the pancakes, heat a lightly oiled griddle or non-stick frying pan over a medium high heat and cook the pancakes in batches, using a small ladle to measure an even amount of liquid for each pancake. The oatcakes must be cooked for two or three minutes on each side. If they brown very quickly, turn the heat down.

Stack the pancakes to help keep them warm and serve them immediately.

You can make a batch in advance and freeze them, stored between layers of baking paper or cling film for up to one month. To reheat, remove paper or cling film, wrap them in foil and place in a low oven for ten minutes.

ingredients

7g fresh yeast

225ml lukewarm milk

75ml lukewarm water

½ tsp sugar

55g strong wholemeal flour

55g strong plain flour

½ tsp salt

115g fine ground oatmeal

Raisin treacle loaf

A low fat, sticky loaf that we love served with salted butter – and one that is so easy to make. Marriages Mill of Chelmsford make an excellent self-raising wholemeal flour from Essex farms that is well worth searching out.

method

Lightly butter a 1 kilo loaf tin and line it with non-stick baking paper.

Preheat the oven to 160C/Gas mark 2-3.

Put the flour, salt, sugar and raisins in a bowl and mix well. Dissolve the treacle in the tepid milk and add it to the bowl, mixing thoroughly. Pour into a lined loaf tin and bake for one hour. Check that the cake is done with a fine skewer: if the skewer comes out clean then the cake is done, if it comes out with soft mixture clinging to it, reduce the heat to 140C/Gas 1-2 and bake the loaf for a further ten minutes, then retest. When the cake is cool, wrap it in foil and keep it for two or three days before eating. Slice the loaf and eat it plain or buttered.

ingredients

280g wholemeal self-raising flour

175g raisins

115g soft dark brown sugar

115g treacle or golden syrup

225ml tepid milk

Easter biscuits

method

Preheat the oven to 200C/Gas mark 6.

Sift the flour, salt and bun spice into a large bowl and grate the butter into the mixture. Using your fingertips, rub in the butter until the mixture resembles breadcrumbs. Stir in the fruit and sugar and add the egg plus enough milk to bind into a firm but not floury dough. Lightly flour your work surface and roll out the mixture to a thickness of about 3mm and cut into 8-10cm rounds using a floured pastry cutter.

Place the biscuits onto baking trays lined with non-stick baking paper and place in the preheated oven for 10-15 minutes. Take the biscuits from the oven and cool on a wire rack. Store in an airtight container.

ingredients

450g plain flour

1 tsp salt

1 tsp bun spice (see page 121)

225g unsalted butter

225g caster sugar

175g sultanas

55g chopped candied peel

2 eggs, beaten

Chocolate tart

This tart is a real favourite. Dark and moist, it is lovely served with fresh raspberries which pair so well with chocolate. Makes one medium tart serving 6-8 people.

method

First, grease a loose-bottomed 20cm tart tin with a little butter, then roll out the pastry to a 25cm circle and use to line the tin, making sure that you press the pastry into all the corners. Leave the pastry overlapping the edges, but reserve a little to fill any gaps later. Chill for 20 minutes, then line the case with non-stick baking paper and fill it with baking beans or dried peas. Place the filled case on a baking tray.

Preheat the oven to 200C/Gas mark 6 and bake the tart case for 25 minutes, or until the pastry is set. Take the tart case out of the oven and carefully remove the beans and paper. Check to see if there are any gaps and use the spare pastry to make repairs, rubbing the raw mixture in just as you would rub filler into the cracks in a wall. Then place the tart case back in the oven for a few minutes until the pastry is dry and browned to your liking: once the filling is added, the pastry will not cook further. Remove the cooked case from the oven and set it to one side while you make the filling.

Put the egg yolks and egg in the bowl of an electric mixer and beat for one minute, then pour in the sugar and beat again until the mixture is very light and fluffy. Melt the chocolate and butter together in a large bowl over a pan of barely simmering water, stirring occasionally until all the chocolate has melted. Transfer the egg mixture to the chocolate, and fold the two together with a large spoon or balloon whisk until well combined. Pour the mixture into the pastry case and bake in the oven for just five minutes at 190C/Gas mark 5. Remove from the oven and leave to cool before slicing with a sharp knife dipped in hot water.

ingredients

200g sweet pastry (see recipe on page 113)

3 egg yolks

2 whole eggs

40g caster sugar

140g unsalted butter

200g plain chocolate, 70-75% cocoa solids, broken into pieces

Orange and lemon tart

The citrus juices balance the sweetness of the pastry perfectly in this tart. Serves 8-12 people

method

First, grease a loose-bottomed 20cm tart tin with a little butter, then roll out the pastry to a 25cm circle and use to line the tin, making sure that you press the pastry into all the corners. Leave the pastry overlapping the edges, but reserve a little to fill any gaps later. Chill for 20 minutes, then line the case with non-stick baking paper and fill it with baking beans or dried peas. Place the filled case on a baking tray.

Preheat the oven to 200C/Gas mark 6 and bake the tart case for 25 minutes, or until the pastry is set. Take the tart case out of the oven and carefully remove the beans and paper. Check to see if there are any gaps and use the spare pastry to make repairs, rubbing the raw mixture in just as you would rub filler into the cracks in a wall. Then place the tart case back in the oven for a few minutes until the pastry is dry and browned to your liking: once the filling is added, the pastry will not cook further. Remove the cooked case from the oven and set it to one side while you make the filling.

Melt the butter in a saucepan over a medium heat, then remove from the stove and add the sugar and rind. Beat the eggs and juice together in a separate bowl then sieve into the mixture. Reduce the oven heat to 140C/Gas mark 2, pour the filling into the tart case and bake the tart for 30 minutes. Check to see if the tart is cooked: if the outer edges are set and the centre is still a little wobbly, it is ready; if the centre is noticeably liquid, leave it for a further ten to fifteen minutes, then check again. Remove the tart from the oven when it is cooked and trim off any surplus pastry. Cool completely before eating.

ingredients

300g sweet pastry
(see recipe on page 113)

For the filling:

200g unsalted butter

200g caster sugar

6 eggs, at room temperature

Zest of 1 lemon and 1 orange, finely grated

Juice of 3 oranges and 6 lemons, sieved

Apple and cinnamon tart Tatin

Serves 6.

method

Put all the pastry ingredients apart from the egg in a food processor and mix well to a coarse, even crumb. Tip into a bowl, then add the egg mixing with a large fork and bring the mixture to a smooth ball, pinching it together lightly. Wrap the pastry in cling film and chill for at least one hour.

Preheat the oven to 220C/Gas mark 7.

Place the butter with the honey and lemon juice in a heavy skillet or a 22cm ovenproof frying pan. Peel and core the apples and cut them into eighths. Arrange the pieces of apple in the bottom of a heavy based pan, and add the honey mixture. Place the pan on a medium heat and leave to caramelise but be careful not to let the mixture burn. Sprinkle with the cinnamon.

Roll the pastry into a round big enough to fit the pan and about 5mm thick. Place it on top of the apples and bake immediately in a hot oven for about 10-15 minutes or until the pastry is crisp. Remove the pan from the oven and loosen the sides of the pastry with a palette knife. Place a large plate upside down on the pan and with one swift movement turn out the tart onto the plate.

ingredients

175g plain flour

55g ground rice

140g cold unsalted butter

Zest of ½ lemon and ½ orange, grated

25g sugar

1 egg, beaten

For the filling:

4 dessert apples, Granny Smith for preference

55g good flavoured British honey

55g unsalted butter

Juice of 2 lemons

1 tsp cinnamon

Cherry and almond filos

method

Put the almonds in a food processor and grind until smooth, then place in a bowl with the rest of the ingredients.

Brush a piece of the filo pastry with some melted butter and then fold in half. Brush again with the melted butter, leaving a dry border of about 2cm around the edge. Spoon on some of the cherry mixture and fold in the two long outside edges, then roll up like a spring roll. Brush with beaten egg and bake in a hot oven (200C/Gas mark 6) for ten minutes or until the pastry is golden. Dust with icing sugar and serve hot or cold.

ingredients

25g roasted flaked almonds

450g stoned cherries

25g soft white bread crumbs

5g pine kernels

55g caster sugar

15g ground cinnamon

A little Kirsch

Filo pastry

Melted butter

Beaten egg for glaze

Icing sugar to dust before serving

Lacy orange tuiles

These lacy biscuits are delicate and fine, but good results can be achieved with care. Non-stick baking paper helps to prevent the biscuits sticking to your baking trays. If you are new to baking you will be advised to bake just one tray at a time – the biscuits cool very quickly and become brittle. So, if you want to shape them by draping them over a rolling pin, you will need to work quickly as soon as they come out of the oven.

method

Combine the almonds, icing sugar and flour in a bowl, then stir in the orange juice and zest. Work in the cooled melted butter, then cover the bowl and place it in the fridge for at least two hours. When you are ready to cook the tuiles, preheat the oven to 180C/Gas mark 4 and line several baking trays with non-stick baking paper. Shape the mixture into small balls, about ¾ tsp each, and flatten them slightly, spacing four or five balls onto your sheets depending on their size.

Bake for about 15-20 minutes. When you take the tuiles out of the oven, lift them off the tray with a palette knife and rest them on a rolling pin to set the shape. When they are set, remove from the rolling pin and store in an airtight tin for up to 2 days. Any broken biscuits can be crushed and used as a topping for ice cream.

ingredients

115g nibbed almonds or chopped flaked almonds

115g icing sugar, sieved

25g plain flour, sieved

25ml orange juice

1 orange zest, finely grated

85g unsalted butter, melted, then cooled to room temperature

Old fashioned shortcake

These slightly soft little cakes are just the thing to serve with strawberries and cream.

method

Preheat the oven to 220C/Gas mark 7.

Sift together the dry ingredients. Rub the butter into the mix, then form into a soft dough using the cream. Knead the dough for a minute and then roll out to a thickness of about 5mm. Using a pastry cutter, cut into rounds.

Line several baking trays with non-stick baking paper and spread the cakes out leaving 2cm between them.

Bake for about ten minutes until the cakes are risen and lightly browned, and sound hollow when tapped. Transfer to a wire cooling rack. When cool, slice them in half and fill with jam and fresh sliced strawberries.

ingredients

115g plain flour

1 rounded tbsp caster sugar

¼ tsp salt

1 tsp baking powder

55g unsalted butter

80ml chilled whipping cream

Desserts

The British climate offers a huge variety of fruit and nuts to use in desserts, though at the restaurant, our most popular summer puddings were based on local berries served simply with Devon clotted cream and home-made biscuits. Chocolate, of course, is universally popular and can be used as the basis for many hot and cold puddings. A favourite is the hot chocolate soufflé you will find here – a really excellent recipe which has the advantage of containing no flour unlike so many soufflé recipes.

When entertaining guests at home, you will find it convenient to have a dessert already made in the fridge or the freezer, and these puddings also fit into the workings of the professional kitchen. In this chapter you will find delicious recipes for tiramisu, lemon icicle and a home-made cream cheese which we like to serve with apple and quince compôte in the autumn when these fruits are at their best. People seem to make fewer puddings themselves these days, but for a special occasion or if you are having friends for lunch, it is nice to make something special. Choose a recipe that complements your main course – a light dish of marinated oranges would be cleansing after a rich red meat or game dish, while a light dish of grilled fish might support a more complex pudding such as the lemon and coconut soufflé.

Blackcurrant and almond tart

The intensity of blackcurrants is unmatched in the fruit garden, and this super tart is a delight in early summer when they are in peak season. In late summer you can substitute brambles, and in winter, cranberries.

Makes 6

method

First, roll out the pastry to line six individual tart cases 8-10cm in diameter, or one 22cm tart tin. Roll the pastry between two sheets of lightly floured non-stick baking paper, then press into the tins, using a lightly floured ball of dough to press it into the edges (this stops the pastry getting warm from the heat of your hands). It is perfectly fine to allow the pastry to hang over the edges of the tart tins a little – this will help stop it collapsing into the tins as they bake, and it can be trimmed once the tarts have cooked and cooled. Reserve any leftover pastry for filling any cracks once the cases are cooked. Chill the tart cases in their tins for 20 minutes in the fridge. Then line each with a sheet of non-stick baking paper and fill with baking beans.

Preheat the oven to 200C/Gas mark 6, and bake the cases for 20 minutes. Then carefully remove the paper lining and check the cases. If there are any cracks, use the leftover dough to fill the gaps, smearing a little raw pastry into the cracks to seal. Return the cases to the oven for 5-10 minutes until they are lightly and evenly browned and crisp. Remove the cases from the oven and keep to one side while you make the filling.

Place the eggs in the bowl of an electric mixer, and beat for three to four minutes. Add the sugar and beat again until the mixture has trebled in volume, then add the almonds and fold them in so that they are mixed evenly. Finally, fold in the blackcurrants and divide the mixture between the tart cases. Return to the oven for 30 minutes until they are lightly browned and just firm to the touch. Trim off any overhanging pastry and cool on a wire rack.

Dust with a little icing sugar and serve with clotted or whipped cream.

ingredients

400g sweet pastry (see page 113)

For the filling:

3 eggs

140g caster sugar

130g ground almonds

450g blackcurrants, picked from their stems

Icing sugar to sprinkle

Passion fruit curd tarts

Many tropical fruits come into their own in the winter months when we are short of a wider variety of locally grown produce. This passion fruit tart makes a refreshing dessert to eat following a rich meal – its aromatic, delicious flavour is just wonderful.

ingredients

400g sweet pastry (see page 113)

For the filling:
15 passion fruit
Juice of 1 lemon
70g caster sugar
100g unsalted butter
1 egg and 1 egg yolk

method

First, roll out the pastry to line six individual tart cases 8-10cm in diameter, or one 22cm tart tin. Roll the pastry between two sheets of lightly floured non-stick baking paper, then press into the tins, using a lightly floured ball of dough to press it into the edges (this stops the pastry getting warm from the heat of your hands). It is perfectly fine to allow the pastry to hang over the edges of the tart tins a little – this will help stop it collapsing into the tins as they bake, and it can be trimmed once the tarts have cooked and cooled. Reserve any leftover pastry for filling any cracks once the cases are cooked. Chill the tart cases in their tins for 20 minutes in the fridge. Then line each with a sheet of non-stick baking paper and fill with baking beans.

Preheat the oven to 200C/Gas mark 6, and bake the cases for 20 minutes. Then carefully remove the paper lining and check the cases. If there are any cracks, use the leftover dough to fill the gaps, smearing a little raw pastry into the cracks to seal. Return the cases to the oven for 5-10 minutes until they are lightly and evenly browned and crisp. Remove the cases from the oven and keep to one side while you make the filling.

Halve the passion fruit and spoon out the contents. Place the flesh in a fine sieve and press through with a spatula so that you extract every bit of the juice. Pour the lemon juice into the sieve, and press through the passion fruit remains – this will bring the remaining flavour with it. Add the caster sugar and the butter to the bowl. Place this mixture into a small stainless steel pan and bring to a simmer over a medium heat. While this is heating, beat the egg and yolk together in a medium bowl. When the passion fruit mixture has come to a simmer, pour onto the egg, stirring constantly. Mix well, then return to the pan over a low heat and cook, stirring constantly, until it thickens and coats the back of a spoon. Immediately pour the mixture through a fine sieve into a cold bowl and cool, stirring occasionally to prevent a skin forming.

When ready to serve, remove the tart cases from their tins, dust the rims with a little icing sugar, and place each on a serving dish. Beat the passion fruit curd to loosen it, and spoon it into the cases. Serve immediately with a little sliced pineapple or mango.

Tiramisu

Serves 6

method

Place a cup full of coffee in a small saucepan over a medium heat and add half the caster sugar. Stir to dissolve the sugar then remove from the heat. Add to the remaining coffee to cool it, then add the Marsala. Place the yolks in the bowl of an electric mixer and beat for one minute, then add the remaining sugar and beat again until the mixture is very thick, pale and creamy.

Place the mascarpone in a large bowl and beat, using a wooden spoon, until it is smooth. Add the egg yolk mixture, fold them together so that they are evenly mixed, then add rum to taste. In a separate bowl whisk the egg whites until they form stiff peaks and fold into the mascarpone.

One by one, dip the sponge fingers briefly in the coffee mixture (if you leave them in too long they will disintegrate) and lay them in the dish until the bottom is covered. Drizzle over a few tablespoons of the coffee so that there are no dry patches and all the fingers are moistened thoroughly. Spread over about a third of the mascarpone mixture and dust with a little cocoa powder. Add another layer of sponge biscuits, dipping in the coffee as before, drizzle with coffee and cover with mascarpone. Repeat this process until you have assembled three layers, then sprinkle over the grated chocolate.

Chill the tiramisu for at least two hours before serving. It will keep in the fridge for up to two days tightly covered with cling film.

ingredients

175g sponge fingers (1 packet)

500g mascarpone cheese

4 large eggs, separated

8 tbsp caster sugar

300ml strong coffee, cold

100ml Marsala

75ml dark rum

2 tbsp cocoa powder

2 tbsp plain chocolate, grated

Chocolate and orange liqueur truffles

A professional cooking chocolate, known as couverture, will be more liquid when melted than ordinary eating chocolate. This makes the chocolate easier to work and excellent as a coating because you can get a really thin, crisp layer. If you are not an orange fan, you can use any liqueur.

Makes about 25

method

Place the cream and sugar in a medium saucepan over a high heat and bring to a gentle simmer, then remove from the heat and add the chocolate. Stir until the chocolate is melted and then add the zest and Grand Marnier, stirring to amalgamate. When the mixture is cool, spoon it onto tray lined with cling film and set the truffles in the freezer. Alternatively pipe them into log-shaped truffles and freeze, then dip in chocolate or cocoa powder and re-freeze. To serve, remove the truffles from the freezer and allow them to thaw in the fridge for an hour before serving.

ingredients

150ml double cream

140g plain chocolate, 70-75% cocoa solids

25g caster sugar

Zest of ½ orange

3 tsp Grand Marnier

135

Iced ginger meringue
with coffee sauce

Serves 8-10

method

Line two large loaf tins with cling film and set aside.

Break the meringues into small pieces but not a powder. Using a large metal spoon, lightly mix together the whipped cream, ginger, coffee and liqueur. Add the meringues and combine gently. Spoon the mixture into the loaf tins and freeze overnight. Slice and serve with the coffee sauce (see below).

ingredients

700ml double cream, lightly whipped

70g preserved stem ginger in syrup, finely chopped

1 tbsp brandy or coffee liqueur

2 tsp instant coffee dissolved in 50ml boiling water, cooled

280g meringue shells

Coffee sauce

Serves 8 (makes about one pint)

method

Put the egg yolks in a bowl and whisk thoroughly, then stir in half the sugar and whisk again. In a medium saucepan, bring the coffee, the milk and the remaining sugar to the boil. Pour the boiling mixture onto the egg yolks, whisking all the time, then return the mixture to the pan over a very low heat. Cook gently, stirring continuously with a wooden spoon, until the custard coats the back of the spoon. Strain and leave to cool. Keep the sauce refrigerated until required.

ingredients

150ml very strong coffee (6 tsp instant coffee dissolved in 150ml boiling water)

40g vanilla sugar (caster sugar infused with a vanilla pod)

300ml milk

4 egg yolks

Apple Charlotte

Serves 6

method

Take six small aluminium pudding moulds, brush the insides with melted butter and dust with a little caster sugar, tipping out any excess. Cut circles from the sliced bread to fit the bottoms of the moulds and a further six circles for the lids. Dip in butter and put in the bottom of the moulds. Cut the remaining bread into strips, dip in butter and line the sides of the moulds, then set aside.

Peel and slice the apples and quince and place in a saucepan with a little water over a medium heat. Cook to a soft, reduced mass with 55g of the remaining butter and 85g sugar, then purée in a food processor and pass through a fine sieve. Add the egg yolks and mix well. Divide between the bread-lined moulds, and top with the lids dipped in butter.

Preheat the oven to 200C/Gas mark 6, and bake the charlottes for about 30 minutes. Leave to cool slightly, then turn out carefully and serve with custard or cream.

ingredients

450g Cox's apples

2 egg yolks

85g caster sugar

115g prepared quince (or increase the apples to 600g)

55g unsalted butter

For the bread moulds:

100g unsalted butter, melted

12 slices stale white bread

25g caster sugar

Autumn fruit salad

Serves 6

method

Place all the ingredients in a large saucepan over a high heat and bring to a simmer. Then reduce the heat and simmer for about 30 minutes or until the fruit is nice and tender. Chill and serve with cream and Old Fashioned Shortcake (see page 131)

ingredients

24 large prunes, stoned

600ml light red wine

4 unpeeled clementines, thickly sliced

4 firm quinces or pears, peeled, cored and quartered

140g honey

8 walnut halves

1 bay leaf

1 inch stick cinnamon

1 vanilla pod

Honey ice cream

Honey can be used in the kitchen in place of sugar – it adds an aromatic, floral sweetness to this ice cream. A local supplier is almost always going to be the best, and local beekeepers can advise you on which honey is the tastiest.

Serves 8

method

Place the honey and milk in a medium saucepan over a high heat. Place the egg yolks in a large bowl and whisk lightly. Keep an eye on the milk and as it rises up the pan to boil, remove from the heat and, while whisking the yolks, pour the milk over and mix thoroughly. The milk should thicken a little, but if it does not, transfer the mixture back to the pan and continue to cook, stirring over a low heat until the custard coats the back of a spoon. Pour through a fine sieve into a large bowl, and allow to cool. When cool, add the cream and mix thoroughly.

You can freeze the mixture either by churning it in an ice cream machine or by pouring into a shallow roasting tin in the freezer. Whisk the mixture every half hour until it begins to freeze and thicken, then transfer it to a food processor and blend into a smooth mass. The whisking and processing will smooth out any ice crystals, and can be repeated as the ice cream freezes and hardens. The ice cream will take about 20 minutes to freeze in a machine, depending on the type, or 12 hours in the freezer. To serve, simply scoop into pretty serving dishes.

ingredients

500ml full fat milk

175g full flavoured British honey

4 egg yolks

300ml double cream

Iced apple and quince soufflé

Serves 8-10

method

Line two large loaf tins with cling film.

Put the egg whites into the bowl of an electric mixer and beat until soft peaks form, then add the sugar and whisk at high speed until thick and meringue-like. In another bowl, whisk the cream until it starts to thicken, then stir in the Calvados. Add half the lemon juice to the fruit purée, taste, and add more as necessary, bearing in mind that the flavour will be dulled by the addition of the cream and egg. Finally fold together the three mixtures, fruit, meringue and cream.

Pour the mixture into the loaf tins and freeze overnight. To serve, lift the frozen loaf from the tin and remove the cling film. Slice in thick slices using a sharp knife dipped in hot water and serve with Langues de chat (see page 115) and some poached pears on the side.

ingredients

450g fruit purée, made from dessert apples and quinces

5 large egg whites

225g caster sugar

600ml double cream

Juice of 1 lemon

50ml Calvados or quince liqueur

Cream cheese

Serves 4-6

method

Warm the milk and cream in a pan to blood temperature, and stir in the rennet. Set aside for half an hour to set. Shape the cream cheese into small moulds, either pierced dariole moulds or china 'cœur à la crème' moulds. Simply line the moulds with muslin, ladle in the cheese and leave to drain overnight. Unfold the muslin and place the cream cheese on a plate. Serve with either fresh berries or a Pear and Quince Compôte (see below).

ingredients

300ml single cream

300ml milk

1tsp rennet

Pear and quince compôte

Serves 6-8

method

Make a syrup with the water, wine and sugar by boiling them together in a stainless steel pan, then add the vanilla pod. Peel the pears and poach them in the syrup until tender, then remove and place them in a dish. Peel the quinces, cut into quarters and poach in the syrup. When they are tender, add them to the pears along with the syrup. Serve cold.

ingredients

4 medium pears, nearly ripe

4 medium quinces, wiped clean

1 vanilla pod, split

130g caster sugar

150ml white wine

150ml water

Seville orange custard

This is an old recipe that has been much used and amended over the years. Sevilles are so special, with a unique flavour that should not be restricted to marmalade. Here it is softened in a lovely delicate custard.

method

Remove the zest from the oranges thinly with a potato peeler and blanch in hot water for five minutes. Drain and put the zest in a blender with the juice from the oranges, the Curaçao and the yolks. Blend to a smooth purée and pour into a large bowl. Heat the cream and sugar together over a medium heat and when it comes to the boil, pour into the orange mixture, stirring as you pour. Return to the pan and cook over a low heat until the mixture has thickened and will coat the back of a spoon. Strain through a fine sieve into a jug.

At this stage it could be served as an accompaniment to Chocolate Marquise (see page 142) or the Chocolate Tart (see page 127). Otherwise divide the custard between four to six ramekins and bake in a bain-marie in the oven for one hour at 140C/Gas mark 2.

Serve hot or cold with a biscuit and decorate with a couple of sweet orange segments.

ingredients

2 Seville oranges

15ml orange Curaçao, triple sec or Grand Marnier

55g caster sugar

300ml single cream

4 egg yolks

Chilled lime soufflé

Serves 6

This light fragrant soufflé can be served following a spicy meal for a welcome coolness. To extract the most juice from the limes, microwave them for 30 seconds once they have been zested. Cut them in half and juice – they will yield much more than when they are cold.

method

Soak the gelatine in cold water.

Put the lime juice, zest and sugar in a small stainless steel pan and dissolve gently, then remove from the heat and cool for ten minutes. Drain the gelatine, squeezing out any water, and add to the pan while still warm. Stir to dissolve and set aside to cool. When the lime mixture is at room temperature, whip the double cream in a large bowl. In a separate bowl, whisk the egg whites until stiff. Fold the lime syrup into the whipped cream using a balloon whisk, then repeat with the egg whites.

Divide between six small glasses or soufflé dishes, and chill for at least four hours before serving.

ingredients

Zest and juice of 4 large limes

3 sheets of gelatine

115g caster sugar

300ml double cream

5 egg whites

Baked quince

Serves 6

method

Wash and dry the quinces to remove any down. Put in an ovenproof dish to fit in a single snug layer and add the honey and water. Cover and place the dish in an oven preheated to 150C/Gas mark 2 for two hours until very tender, basting with the juices. If at any time the quinces appear to be dry, add a little more water, but allow the mixture to reduce to a light syrup.

Serve while still just warm with cream, custard or ice cream.

ingredients

6 medium quinces

2 tbsp honey

150ml water

Lemon icicle

This recipe, a favourite at the restaurant, came from Morella Coiley, mother to Nick, our head chef for many years and a great friend. It is simplicity itself.

Serves 8-10

method

Pour a little water into two small loaf tins, then drain them. Line each with a piece of cling film – the water helps it to stick.

In a large bowl over a pan of hot water, whisk the eggs and sugar until very thick. Remove the bowl from the heat and continue whisking until cold. In a separate bowl whisk together the cream, lemon juice and zest until soft peaks form. Carefully fold the two mixtures together, pour into the tins and freeze for 12 hours.

To serve, dip the tins in a basin of hot water and turn the icicle out onto a clean chopping board. Remove the cling film and slice using a sharp knife dipped in hot water. Serve with raspberry sauce (see page 149).

ingredients

300ml double cream

3 eggs

125g caster sugar

Zest and juice of two lemons, finely grated

Chocolate Marquise

A very rich frozen pudding.

method

Melt the chocolate and butter in a bowl over hot water and beat until smooth. Set aside to cool. In a separate bowl, whisk the egg yolks and 55g of the sugar until thick and pale. In another bowl, whisk the egg whites until stiff and then whisk in the remaining sugar. Mix the yolk mixture into the chocolate and then fold in the egg whites. Pour the mixture into a loaf tin lined with cling film and freeze.

When ready to eat, remove the Marquise from the tin and carefully peel away the cling film. Serve in thin slices with Raspberry Sauce (page 149) or Seville orange custard (page 140) and Langues de chat (page 115).

ingredients

225g 70% plain chocolate

115g unsalted butter

2 large eggs, separated

85g icing sugar

Hot chocolate soufflé

Serves 6

Melted butter and caster sugar for lining the dishes

method

Prepare six individual soufflé dishes by brushing the insides with melted butter. To help the soufflés rise, brush the insides with vertical strokes from bottom to rim so that the butter goes to the very top of the dish in a straight line. Then dust with caster sugar, making sure the insides are all coated, and tip out any excess.

Melt the chocolate, brandy, water and sugar in a bowl in a bain-marie. Remove from the heat and mix well. Add the egg yolks and mix again. In a bowl, whisk the egg whites until they form stiff peaks and fold them into the chocolate mixture. Pour into prepared soufflé dishes and cook for about ten minutes in an oven preheated to 220C/Gas mark 7. When cooked, dust with icing sugar and serve immediately with cream or home-made ice cream.

ingredients

100g caster sugar

225g dark chocolate

50ml brandy

100ml water

6 eggs, separated

Strawberry iced soufflé

Serves 8

method

Have ready a large loaf tin lined with cling film, or a 1-litre bomb mould.

Hull the strawberries and purée in a liquidizer with 50g of the sugar. Sieve the purée into a large bowl. Place the egg whites in the bowl of an electric mixer. Beat on high speed for one minute, then add the rest of the caster sugar and beat again until the mixture is thick and glossy and forms firm peaks.

While the egg white is beating, whip the cream until it forms soft peaks and fold in the liqueur. Fold the strawberry purée and cream together using a balloon whisk, then fold in the egg white and spread into the loaf tin or bomb mould. Freeze overnight, then cut with a sharp knife dipped in hot water. Serve with strawberries mixed with a little strawberry purée and Langues de chat (see page 115).

ingredients

500g ripe strawberries

200g caster sugar

3 egg whites

450ml double cream

3 tbsp strawberry or orange liqueur

Gooseberry cream jelly

Serves 6

method

Place the water, wine and sugar in a saucepan over a medium to high heat. Allow the mixture to simmer until the sugar is dissolved, then add the gooseberries. Allow the pan to come back to a simmer, then reduce the heat and allow the gooseberries to cook gently. When they are just cooked, tip the mixture through a sieve supported over a large bowl. Add three sheets of gelatine to the liquid and stir to dissolve, then taste and add a little more sugar if required. Divide between six nice serving glasses of about 150ml - capacity. Place the glasses in the fridge to chill and set.

Put the gooseberries in a blender and purée well. Add the remaining gelatine, stirring well, then taste and add a little more sugar if required. Chill thoroughly, then whip the cream and fold in the gooseberries. Top the chilled, set jelly, with the gooseberry and cream mixture, dividing it equally between the glasses. Chill for at least four hours before serving.

If elderflowers are in season keep a little jelly back and make a top layer with tiny sprigs of elderflower in the jelly (see above).

ingredients

500g slightly ripe green or red gooseberries, topped and tailed

125ml water

125ml white wine or apple juice

120g caster sugar

6 sheets gelatine, soaked in cold water

125ml double cream

Caramel rice

A vanilla-scented, light mixture of cooked rice just set with gelatine. The rice adds a pleasant contrast to the sublime creaminess of the mousse.

Serves 6

method

First make the caramel. Place a small heavy pan over a medium heat and add the caster sugar. Heat without stirring, shaking the pan gently until the sugar melts and turns an even brown colour. Remove the pan from the heat and very carefully add a little hot water to slacken the caramel, rotating the pan. Pour a little caramel into each of six dariole moulds or ramekins. Take care as the pan will be very hot.

Place the rice, vanilla sugar, milk and cream into a saucepan over a medium heat and bring to a simmer. Reduce the heat to low and stir occasionally, for about one and a quarter or one and a half hours, until the rice is completely tender and the mixture has thickened.

Let the rice cool until it is warm but no longer hot, then add the egg yolks and soaked gelatine, squeezed to remove excess water, and mix thoroughly. Now let the rice cool to room temperature, then whip the egg whites to firm peaks and fold into the rice mixture. Divide the mixture between the ramekins and chill for at least four hours, or overnight if possible.

To serve, dip the moulds into hot water, and turn out onto cold serving plates. Serve with summer berries or poached apricots.

ingredients

60g caster sugar

40g round grain rice

40g vanilla sugar (caster sugar infused with a vanilla pod)

300ml milk

300ml single cream

2 eggs, separated

2 sheets gelatine, soaked in cold water

Apple and cinnamon fritters

Serves 4

method

Sift the flour and salt into a basin and make a hollow in the middle. Mix the egg yolk with a little cider and pour into the well. Gradually add the rest of the cider and mix into a smooth batter. If it goes lumpy, pass it through a sieve. Cover the batter and set aside to rest for an hour or two.

When ready, turn your deep fat fryer to 190C or heat a 3cm layer of oil in a deep frying pan and monitor the temperature with a probe. Whip the egg whites until stiff and fold them into the batter. Dip the slices of apple into the batter and drop into the oil.

Fry the fritters in batches for three to five minutes turning half way through. Drain them on kitchen paper and keep the first batch warm in a low oven (140C/Gas mark 1) until they are all cooked. Dredge in cinnamon and sugar and serve immediately with honey ice cream (see page 135).

ingredients

140g plain flour

1 egg, separated

300ml dry cider

1 pinch salt

4 Cox's apples, peeled, cored and thickly sliced

2 tbsp caster sugar and 1 tsp cinnamon, mixed, for dredging

Spiced marinated oranges

Serves 8

method

Heat the wine, spices, sugar and currants in a large saucepan over a high heat, the boil and reduce to about a quarter of a pint or 150ml. Remove from the heat, add the Grand Marnier and port and set aside to cool.

Place each orange in turn on a tray, and cut a disc from the top and bottom. Using a serrated or very sharp knife, cut down the sides of the oranges, removing the skin and all the white pith. Then slice each segment of orange out from the membrane, sectioning all the fruit in turn. Reserve any juices and add to the spiced wine mixture.

Arrange the sections of orange in a nice serving dish and pour over the wine mixture. Chill for at least four hours before serving. Excellent after a rich game dish.

ingredients

10 medium oranges

600ml fruity red wine

8 tbsp caster sugar

1 cinnamon stick

2 cardamom pods

55g currants

125ml port

30ml Grand Marnier

Lemon and coconut soufflé

A special mixture that balances the sharpness of the citrus fruit with the rich coconut.

Serves 4

method

Prepare four individual soufflé dishes by brushing the insides with melted butter. To help the soufflés rise, brush the insides with vertical strokes from bottom to rim so that the butter goes to the very top of the dish in a straight line. Then dust with caster sugar, making sure the insides are all coated, and tip out any excess.

In a medium pan, heat together the coconut and milk over a low to medium heat, stirring to combine. In another pan, melt the butter and add the flour, allowing the two to cook together for a few minutes. Then add the milk a little at a time to make a smooth sauce, beating well between additions. Then add 25g of the caster sugar. Cook the mixture for two or three minutes until it is smooth, glossy and no longer tastes of flour. Set aside to cool. When cool add the yolks, lemon zest and juice.

At this stage the mixture can be set aside for up to 24 hours. When your guests are ready, preheat the oven to 160C/Gas mark 2. Beat the egg whites with a balloon whisk until they form stiff peaks. Beat the coconut and lemon mixture and stir in a spoonful of egg white to help loosen it. Fold in the remaining whites and fill the soufflé dishes to the rim. Clean the dishes of any spills and place the dishes on a baking tray. Bake for 6-8 minutes or until they are well risen and browned evenly on the surface. Remove from the oven and dust lightly with icing sugar. Serve with lemon and coconut sauce (see below).

ingredients

55g creamed coconut, grated

150ml full fat milk

25g unsalted butter

25g plain flour

85g caster sugar

4 eggs, separated

Zest and juice of ½ lemon

Melted butter and caster sugar for lining the dishes

Lemon and coconut sauce

Use this to complement the soufflé.

method

Melt all the ingredients together in a small stainless steel pan over a low heat and keep warm until ready to serve with the soufflé.

ingredients

Zest and juice of two lemons

115g caster sugar

25g unsalted butter

55g creamed coconut, grated

Rhubarb and frangipane slice

Serves 6

method

Lightly dust your work surface with a little flour and roll out the pastry to a rectangle about 18x35cms. Trim the edges to neaten them, then cut a 2cm strip from each side of the rectangle and set these aside.

Line a large baking tray with non-stick baking paper and carefully lift the pastry onto it. Prick the pastry all over with a fork, then brush a little cold water along each edge. Using the reserved trimmings, make a border around the rectangle. Set the pastry aside to chill in the fridge for 15 minutes while you prepare the frangipane.

Place the butter in a large bowl and beat with a wooden spoon until it is light and creamy. Add the caster sugar and beat again, then add the egg. Mix well together, then add the ground almonds and the flour. Remove the pastry from the fridge and spread the almond mixture on the surface, being careful not to get any on the border.

Preheat the oven to 200C/Gas mark 6.

Lay the rhubarb out on a board and cut the pieces so that they fit just inside the pastry border. Lay the rhubarb on the surface of the almond mixture and press the pieces lightly into it. Bake in the oven for 20 minutes until evenly browned and well risen. Turn off the heat and leave the tart in the oven with the door ajar for a further ten minutes, then remove from the oven and transfer to a wire cooling rack.

Place the apricot jam in a small saucepan over a medium heat. Add 2 tbsp water, bring to a gentle simmer and sieve to remove any lumps. Brush the tart with the glaze, and serve when just cool with Jersey cream.

ingredients

375g puff pastry (see page 114)

50g unsalted butter at room temperature

50g caster sugar

50g ground almonds

½ tbsp plain flour

1 medium egg, beaten

375g rhubarb, trimmed and wiped

4 tbsp apricot jam

Raspberry sauce

Serves 8

method

Place the raspberries, sugar and water in a liquidizer and blend to a smooth purée. Sieve to remove any pips and sharpen with a squeeze of lemon juice.

ingredients

250g raspberries

100g caster sugar

50ml water

Lemon juice

Notes

Notes

Notes

Index

Index

Suppliers

Loch Duart Salmon

Badcall Salmon House, Scourie, Lairg, Sutherland, IV27 4TH
Telephone 01674 660161 Email janeanne.mackie@lochduartsalmon.com

This, pioneering farm rears salmon in low stocked enclosures and feeds a sustainable food giving the salmon a firm, delicious flesh.

Summer Isles Foods

Summer Isles Foods, Achiltibuie, Ullapool, Ross-shire, IV26 2YG
Telephone 01854 622353 Email sales@summerislesfoods.co.uk

Located north west of Ullapool in Achiltibuie, Summer Isles Foods produce a unique range of different styles of smoked salmon, and you can choose from a selection of smoked fish including award winning Achiltibuie kippers.

Dunkeld Smoked Salmon.

Springwells Smokehouse, Brae Street, Dunkeld, Perthshire PH8 0BA
Telephone 01350 727639 Email enq@dunkeldsmokedsalmon.com

Multi award winning specialist smokers of high welfare farmed (including Loch Duart) and wild smoked salmon throughout the UK.

Brown and Forrest Smokery

Bowdens Farm, Hambridge, Langport, Somerset TA10 OBP
Telephone 01458 250875 Email info@smokedeel.co.uk

Brown and Forrest is a family run smokery. Started nearly 30 years ago in Somerset they produce some of the finest smoked eel and salmon as well as a whole range of delicious smoked food such as chicken, duck, lamb and trout.

W & H Marriage and Sons Ltd

Chelmer Mills, New Street, Chelmsford, Essex, CM1 1PN
Telephone 01245 354455 Email floursales@marriagesmillers.co.uk

Family run flour millers since 1824. Marriage's produce award winning quality flours, including organic varieties and traditionally milled stone-ground wholemeal bread making flour.

Reid Wines

The Mill, Marsh Lane, Hallatrow, Bristol BS39 6EB
Telephone 01761 452645 Fax 01761 453645 email reidwines@aol.com

Fine wines, depth of knowledge and infectious enthusiasm were the traits we so admired when we dealt with the late founder, Bill Baker. The company continues to flourish and fulfil all our expectations under the stewardship of David Boobbyer. Independent merchants offering an eclectic range of old, rare and everyday drinking wines

Christopher Piper Wines Ltd

Silver Street, Ottery St. Mary, Devon, EX11 1DB
Telephone 01404 814139 Email sales@christopherpiperwines.co.uk

Established in 1979, they are a Devon based, independent wine merchant offering expert opinion on a wide ranging selection of quality wines. They supply both Trade and Public throughout the UK. A good service that begins and ends with quality.

Notes

Ovens

If we were to make these recipes in six different ovens, we would get six slightly different results: such is the variation in temperature and power between models and fuel types. Temperatures are given throughout in Centigrade and as gas marks, and a conversion chart for Fahrenheit is given as an appendix below. It is useful, we think, especially when baking, to have an oven thermometer that sits inside the oven that will give accurate readings at all times. This will be particularly helpful when using a convection or fan oven, as these tend to run a few degrees hotter than a traditional oven. If you are using a convection or fan oven, reduce the cooking temperature by 5-10C to get an even result.

Conversion chart (Fahrenheit, Celsius and Gas Mark)

Degrees Fahrenheit	Degrees Celsius	Gas Mark	Description
125	110	1/4	Very slow
250	120/130	1/2	Very slow
275	140	1	Slow
300	150	2	Slow
325	160/170	3	Moderate
350	180	4	Moderate
375	190	5	Moderately hot
400	200	6	Moderately hot
425	220	7	Hot
450	230	8	Hot
475	240	9	Very hot

Recipes

All the recipes in this book have been used for many years, both in the restaurant kitchen and in our own homes. All the ingredients we have used are available today. A few, such as sweetbreads, may require a little searching out, but most are easily sourced from local shops and suppliers. In most case we have given a rough indication of how many portions each recipe makes, but of course in reality this will depend on how hungry you and your family are. We would encourage you to read the recipe methods before you embark on cooking any of the dishes in order to get an idea of how long each will take. Most can be made and served on the same day, but a few, such as gravadlax and bresaola, require several days, or weeks.

Ingredients

At home, and in the restaurant, we favour the best ingredients we can source: those with the best flavour. So, we would recommend British, locally produced ingredients that are either freshly harvested or sold from shops that you have confidence in, particularly when it comes to meat and fish. Butter, in our case, is always British, more usually local to our homes. Imported, salted butter has a very short shelf life and turns rancid quickly. Lightly salted, or unsalted butter is a good default ingredient, allowing you to salt to a level that you prefer. We have used large eggs unless specified, and unbleached, British flour in the main.

All store cupboard ingredients should be kept cool. One of the downsides of modern, centrally heated homes is that they are almost certainly too hot, meaning that ingredients – both fresh and dried – have a shorter shelf life. Buy your ingredients in small quantities as you need them, unless you have a larder fridge, chest freezer or pantry in which to store them.

A big thank you

Thanks, of course, to Adam White who has given so much support and printing expertise to this project, and enthusiasm by the bucket load. Also, thanks to Michael Murray King, who gave up his free time to make such lovely photographs.

Robert Matthews supported us all throughout, offering sensible advice, washing up, and offering calming words when they were most needed.

Thanks, particularly to Sandra Baker for reading, checking, and looking after our admin during this project.

Mark Griffiths gave much time and effort to the lovely, clean design, and Mike Weare who edited and proof read the text.

To all the staff, suppliers and customers of The Carved Angel, who are too numerous to mention, but without whom, this project would have not happened.

And, finally, to all of the team at Save the Children who strive, fight, and achieve so much around the world for humanity.